WEST COAST \

OBAN TO MALLAIG

including Fort William and

MULL

WEST COAST WALKS

OBAN TO MALLAIG

including Fort William and

MULL

Pamela Clark

KITTIWAKE

Published by
Kittiwake Press
3 Glantwymyn Village Workshops, Machynlleth,
Montgomeryshire SY20 8LY

First edition 2000

Every care has been taken to make the information,
walk descriptions and maps as accurate as possible
but neither the author or the publisher can accept any
responsibility for errors, however caused.
The countryside is always changing and land ownership
may alter access, so there will inevitably be alterations
to some aspects of these walks in future. If you would
like to help keep this book up to date, please send
your comments to the above address.

Please remember that much land is private. Inclusion
in this book does not imply any right of public access.

Roads and tracks indicated are not necessarily
rights of way. If in doubt, seek permission first.

Produced on an Apple Macintosh using Adobe Photoshop,
Macromedia Freehand and QuarkXPress.

The typeface is Melior.

Film output by
WPG, Welshpool, Montgomeryshire

Printed by
MFP Design & Print, Manchester

A catalogue record for this book may be found in the British Library

ISBN 1 902302 02 8
1/1/4.00

Cover photographs: Main picture: Sgurr Ghiubhsachain;
inset: The author above Glencoe

INTRODUCTION

The west coast of Scotland between Oban and Mallaig is one of the most dramatic and beautiful parts of Europe. A land indented by long sea lochs with a myriad of islands and fringed with quiet white-sand beaches or stunning rocky shores and precipitous cliffs, leading inland to empty moorland, deeply carved glacial valleys and high rugged mountains sweeping down to the sea. Largely due to the Highland Clearances of the 18th and 19th centuries, when people were callously evicted to make way for sheep, it is a large empty quarter, with a generally sparse population who eke out a living, mainly from tourism, fishing, crofting and forestry. Its relative remoteness has resulted in a tremendous range of wildlife thriving, unequalled elsewhere in Britain. With a great variety of flora and fauna habitats, found often in close proximity, botanists too will find a paradise. Anglers will be spoilt for choice in their search for excellent freshwater and sea fishing, and experienced yachtsmen will find a surfeit of challenging waters.

With a lack of roads across much of the region, the only way to really explore is on foot or by boat. The purpose of this book is to be both a tourist and walking guide, catering for all; from the visitor who likes the occasional easy stroll to the hardened hillwalker who likes to be more of a general tourist on a rest day from the mountains. A number of ascents of Munros and Corbetts have been included. For those unfamiliar with these terms, a Munro is one of the 284 mountains in Scotland over 3000 feet, first surveyed and listed by Sir Hugh Munro in 1891. A Corbett is one of the 221 hills between 2500 – 3000 feet with a reascent of at least 500 feet on all sides between adjoining hills. Ticking off all the Corbetts has not gained the popularity that climbing all the Munros has (Munro bagging) and subsequently makes for much quieter hills but no less outstanding viewpoints. Along with many gentle walks, some lesser hill ascents are also described, which provide equally fine views.

The coast has been divided up into two sections, firstly from Oban to Fort William and secondly west to Mallaig and south to Moidart, Ardnamurchan, Morvern and Ardgour. For each section, the text and maps describe all the places of interest, as if on a guided tour. Essential tourist information is also given on what and where non-walking activities can be enjoyed, and on availability of public transport.

Within the text and listed in the appendix, are the locations of Tourist Information Offices in the area. These are invaluable, being the most up to date sources of local information on available accommodation and restaurants, times of public transport, availability of day excursions, boat charters and opening times of tourist facilities. The appendix also has useful phone numbers for a large range of outdoor enthusiasts.

Over fifty scenic walking routes are described in the book, ranging from half hour strolls to full day strenuous walks in the mountains and along the coast. Virtually every hard walk, also has an easier option suggested, for the less energetic, within the same locality. No-one on their holiday should be at a loss for where to go for a rewarding walk. The majority provide views of the sea at some point, although a few keep to sheltered forest trails and glens where the main objective usually, is to reach a beautiful waterfall: ideal destinations when the weather is too inclement for the coasts and hills. The Isle of Mull has been included, though only in the walks section, having been covered in the sister publication, *The Western Islands Handbook.* However, many of the tourist sites are included within the text of the walks. Mull is easily visited on a day trip by those staying in Oban, although to see the best of the island, it is worth staying there for a few days.

All of the easier walking routes follow tracks and paths, though many of the hillwalks have long pathless sections. Unlike in England and Wales, very few Scottish mountains have cairned or easy to follow paths all the way up, adding to the challenge and sense of adventure. Cairns are only usually found on the highest points. Hillwalkers therefore, must be competent in the use of map and compass. Also, unlike most of their southern and eastern counterparts, most hillwalks in western Scotland start at or close to sea level, so a certain level of fitness is required. Another difference is the lack of bridges across many rivers, so it is advisable to be familiar with river crossing techniques. Snow can linger on the summits well into April and occasionally into May, so competence with ice axe and crampons will be required at such times. All walkers should carry good waterproof clothing and wear stout footwear. In addition, hillwalkers should carry a spare top, map, compass, torch, whistle, basic first-aid kit and adequate food and drink. It is advisable to leave word of your route with someone and expected time back, particularly if hillwalking alone.

It is important to bear in mind that the weather can change very rapidly and dramatically. It is not unusual to experience all four seasons within a few hours! The west coast climate is generally mild and wet and unpredictable. From the author's experience (and to some extent, statistics back this up), usually the best time to visit is from late April to the end of June, when in most years there is a relative drought lasting 6 – 8 weeks. There is often a long settled spell too in October. At other times you will generally experience far more wet days than dry, though just occasionally, there is drought for much of the summer. Late April and May are particularly attractive, not only with the drier weather and very long daylight hours but because of the lack of midges. These wee pests do not usually start biting until early June. In late spring too, the woods are carpeted with bluebells and primroses and the vibrant greens of the valleys contrast with the northern corries and mountain summits still fringed white with snow. Autumn is particularly beautiful, with the coming of the first summit snows, the rowan trees in full fruit and the trees and bracken turning colour. The midges also are dying away.

Roads are often narrow and can be single track, requiring careful considerate driving. By avoiding the height of summer, driving is much more pleasurable. Allow plenty of time for your journey and be aware that petrol stations are often far apart and generally closed in the evening and on Sundays. If circumstances dictate that you have to visit during busier July and August, by using this book, you can get well off the beaten track and find natural tranquillity. Just remember the waterproofs and insect repellent!

As you explore the area, take care to respect the land and its people, flora and fauna. This remains one of the most unspoilt areas of Europe. Long may it remain so.

Pam Clark

TOURIST INFORMATION

OBAN

Oban is a very busy tourist centre, being an ideal base for exploring much of Argyll and an important ferry terminal serving the Isles of Mull (see **walks 21-31**), Colonsay, Tiree, Coll, Lismore, Kerrera and Barra. Sheltered by the Isle of Kerrera (see **walk 6**), it lies in a crescent bay surrounded by low, steep hills, looking out onto the beautiful Firth of Lorn and Sound of Mull. Many of the houses and hotels are Victorian, built to cope with the influx of tourists following the coming of the steam boats around 1850 and the railway in 1880. Rail services to Glasgow have survived the recent threats of closure although the number of daily trains has been reduced to three. The town is dominated by the Victorian edifice of **McCaig's Tower,** a dark grey granite mini Coliseum, built in 1897 by Oban banker, John Stuart McCaig, to ease unemployment amongst local masons. The proposed art gallery and family monument was never completed. Reached by a steep ten minute walk from town, or by car or bus, it affords a superb view across Oban Bay to Mull. An even finer viewpoint is from the top of Pulpit Hill overlooking the South Pier.

There are a variety of activities for tourists to enjoy (Tourist Information Centre, George Square *open daily Jan – Dec*). Oban is a busy fishing port and a major yachting and diving centre. Oban lifeboat is one of the busiest in Britain. The challenging waters off the west coast are not for unaccompanied novices. For boat hire, contact Borroboats, Gallanach Road (01631 563292). Anglers can enjoy good pier and sea fishing for conger, codling, sea trout, mackerel and skate. For permits and information on trout and salmon fishing in the region, contact Anglers Corner 01631 566374. Day cruises can be arranged to Duart Castle, Mull, Staffa, Iona and local seal colonies. A popular Highland Games takes place on the *last Thursday in August.*

The only good beach in the area with safe swimming and water sports is 2 miles north at **Ganavan,** (also a restaurant and children's' play area). From Ganavan, it is possible to take a rough footpath for 2 miles northward to Dunstaffnage, with excellent views en route to Lismore and Mull. The narrow, winding road to Ganavan passes the modern granite Catholic Cathedral of St Columba and leads in 0.75 mile to **Dunollie Castle.** Built around the 7th century, the original fortification was a stronghold of the Kings of Lorn, at a time when Scotland was still divided into a number of small kingdoms. Burnt by the Irish in 698, it was rebuilt and became the seat of the MacDougalls. Abandoned after the 1745 Jacobite Rising, four storeys still remain. The flat walk to Dunollie from town is delightfully scenic to seaward. Grey herons often feed in the small bay just below the castle.

If looking for an escape from the rain, **Oban Distillery** in Stafford Street offers tours (*Mon – Sat*). On the North Pier, the renowned **World in Miniature** (*Easter – Oct*) houses intricate rooms and furniture on a scale of 1 inch to 1 foot, dioramas and paintings. On Railway Quay **Caithness Glass** have a factory shop and interpretative exhibition. **Leisure Centres** caters for swimming, squash, tennis, table tennis, snooker and bowls. There is a small **cinema** and the **Corran Halls** regularly stages family shows during the summer.

KILMORE TO EASDALE

Leaving Oban by Glencruitten Road, passes the challenging 18 hole golf course with extremely narrow fairways. In 2 miles you reach the Connel - Kilmore road and **Oban Rare Breeds Park** which houses rare farm animal breeds and deer in a fine setting (*late March – Oct*).

Turning right onto the Kilmore road, the narrow road winds over a low pass then descends through old oakwood to enchanting **Loch Nell** (see **walk 2**). Close to its south west corner are several Bronze Age cairns and a fine example of a prehistoric 'snake mound', possibly a relic of Pagan worship. Unfortunately, barbed wire fencing makes access difficult. *'Loch of the swans* is well named. Swans still nest here on a tiny islet close to shore.

Half a mile along River Nell, a no through road forks left for **Glen Feochan** (see **walks 3 & 4**). Parking is very limited in the glen and passing places poor, so not recommended unless planning to walk or fish. A path a mile from the road end leads to Loch Nant in 5 miles, a hill reservoir stocked with trout and popular with energetic anglers. The 'major' road, reaches the A816 Oban – Lochgilphead road in half a mile, 5 miles south of Oban.

Turning south along Loch Feochan, **Glen Feochan House Gardens** (*March – Oct*), include collections of rare trees, prolific rhododenrons and beautiful herbaceous borders. Further along the loch, **The Scottish Salmon Centre** offers an interactive exhibition centre and audio visual show (*Easter – Nov*). Alternatively, test your driving skills at the grass track rally karting. Nearby at Kilninver, a road branches off to **Seil Island** and **Easdale.** Combined with **Loch Nell**, it makes for a very pleasant easy day outing from Oban. Seil is actually only separated from the mainland by a narrow, viciously humped old stone Telford bridge, 'The Bridge Over The Atlantic'. Rural scenes give way to fine coastal views as you follow the narrow road to the small village of **Ellanbeich**, often referred to as Easdale along with **Easdale Island**, a short ferry ride away. There is an historical map of the island at the interesting folk museum (*open April – Oct*). It takes about 30 minutes to walk around the island. Slate quarrying was a major industry here until World War 1. Local arts and crafts have now taken over. The area has also been popular for location filming by film and TV producers since the 1950s.

Returning towards Oban, north of Kilmore, a road branches left to **Ardoran Pier** via Lerags and **Kilbride (walk 5)**. A marine sports centre at **Ardoran** caters for windsurfers and yachtsmen and boat hire is available. The road passes the restored 16th century Lerags Cross and the ruins of Kilbride church dating from 1706, the burial place of successive MacDougall chiefs since 1737.

OBAN TO LOCH AWE

Heading north out of Oban, a minor road at Dunbeg leads to the well preserved and imposing 13th century **Dunstaffnage Castle** (*open March – Oct*). The 60-foot curtain walls stand in a grand setting, looking out to Lismore, Morven and Appin. It was built on the site of the ancient capital of Dalriada which housed the Stone of Destiny until moved to Scone by Kenneth MacAlpin`, the first King of a united Scotland. Closeby, a yachting marina offers boat charters, water ski-ing and windsurfing.

Five miles from Oban, lies the village of **Connel.** Like Oban, much of its tourist accommodation stems from the coming of the railway. Its name derives from the Gaelic, *'conghail', tumultuous flood.* The village overlooks the Falls of Lora at the mouth of Loch Etive. The falls are rapids rather than a true fall; a shallow seawater maelstrom at ebb tide when Loch Etive races into the Atlantic. During the last Ice Age, this was a rock lip at the end of the Etive glacier.

The A85 turns east along the well wooded and beautiful **Loch Etive.** Three miles from Connel, **Achnacloich Gardens** (*April – mid June*), are noted for the fine displays of rhododendrons, azaleas and primulas. The main road continues to **Taynuilt.** Turn left to the pier for a wonderful view. In summer, boat trips leave here and cruise up the roadless section of the spectacular loch. With luck you may spy seals which frequent these waters. (Loch Etive Cruises 01866 822430). There are delightful picnic spots nearby. Also **Bonawe Furnace,** an industrial heritage site (*April –Sept*) well worth a visit. It is a well preserved and restored charcoal fuelled iron furnace that saw service from 1752 – 1875. Taynuilt's 9 hole golf course is infinitely more user friendly for novices than Oban.

Just beyond the village, a road forks right for Kilchrenan and the western shore of Loch Awe. Two miles along Glen Nant, there is a popular picnic spot at the Tailor's Leap, a 40 foot fall. The initially fine vistas towards Ben Cruachan rapidly deteriorate, the blanket coniferous plantations restricting lochside scenes considerably. Inverliever Forest however, around the environs of **Dalavich,** offers interesting sheltered walks when the weather is too stormy for the coasts and hills (**walk 1**). The approach to Dalavich from Kilmelford to the west, is scenically much finer.

Keeping on the A85, 2 miles east of Taynuilt, a twisting single track road turns off for Inverawe where there is a salmon farm and smokery with an exhibition and nature trail, casting tuition and trout fishing. From the road end there is an easy walk along Loch Etive (**walk 13c**). The main road continues through the Pass of Brander a dramatic geological fault line, dominated by the sprawling mass of Ben Cruachan to the left (**walk 7**) and steep screes to the right, tumbling into the narrows of the loch. The narrow defile is named after Robert the Bruce's successful ambush of MacDougall of Lorn in 1308. The latter escaped, though many of his men perished as they tried to escape from the narrow confines of the pass, across the River Awe. Bruce subsequently successfully besieged Dunstaffnage Castle and gained control of Argyll. The MacDougalls thus lost much of their territory and the Campbells of Loch Awe became hereditary keepers of the castle.

In poor weather, **Cruachan Power Station and Visitor Centre** offer tourists an interesting escape (*daily, Easter – Nov*). Minibuses run for nearly a mile underground to the huge cavern housing the hydro electric turbines. In high summer, go early to avoid the queues.

From **Lochawe village**, 2 miles beyond, one can cruise on the loch. St Conan's Church only dates from 1886 but it is a fascinating and bizarre mix of architectural styles. It contains some fragments of Iona Abbey and there is a memorial chapel to Robert the Bruce.

Leaving the village, the B8077 forks off to lonely **Glen Strae** whilst the A85 continues towards Dalmally (see easier options to **walk 8**) past the extremely photogenic **Kilchurn Castle.** Built by the Campbells in 1440, it is well preserved inspite of much of its slate and stone having gone into the building of local housing since 1770. Across the road is Dalmally golf course, laid out in a wonderful setting with equally wonderful cheap green fees. The village of **Dalmally** itself, is a mile to the east. A popular village with anglers and walkers, it is well served by both bus and rail links with Glasgow. There is a fine example of an 18th century 'round' church on a small island in the river.

Closeby, the A819 heads off to **Inverary,** a popular scenic excursion from Oban. Inverary is an attractive Georgian town with an award winning reconstruction of a 19th century jail and courthouse (*open all year*) and a grandiose 18th century castle, home to the Duke of Argyll (*April – Oct*). The Episcopal Church is famed for its beautiful bells. The **Arctic Penguin,** an iron ship, houses interesting Maritime exhibits with hands on activities. Two miles to the south is **Argyll Wildlife Centre** on Loch Fyne and in a further 3 miles, **Auchindrain Museum** is an original West Highland township which reconstructs farming life in days gone by (*April – Sept*).

The B840 leaves the A819 to follow the eastern shore of **Loch Awe.** When the trees permit, there are enchanting views to the mountains dominating the many small bays, islands and deciduous wooded peninsulas. Just beyond Blarghour farmhouse, some 14 miles down the loch, a spectacular waterfall dropping vertically for some 100 feet can be viewed by following the left bank upstream. A lower falls plunges 26 feet. Boat hire is available at Portsonachan. The loch offerring anglers superb trout and salmon fishing. For a circular tour back to Oban, one can continue down the loch to reach the A816 Lochgilphead – Oban road just south of Ford. Heading northward, Loch Melfort is particularly attractive. **Arduaine Gardens** at the mouth of the loch, are worthy of exploration. Famed for its outstanding collection of rhododendrons, azaleas and magnolias, it also supports many other interesting trees, shrubs and herbaceous perennials and boasts attractive water features (*daily 0930 – sunset*).

CONNEL, ARDCHATTAN AND APPIN

At Connel, the A828 crosses the Falls of Lora by way of an impressive 1903 steel cantilever bridge. On the far side, a road branches eastward along the attractive north shore of Loch Etive to Ardchattan and Bonawe. **Ardchattan Priory** was founded in 1230. The priory church was burnt in 1645 and the priory itself in 1654. The Laird of Ardchattan having sided with the Royalists during the Civil War. The adjacent gardens of shrubs and herbaceous plants are open to the public (*April – Oct*). The road ends at Bonawe Quarry where granite has been extracted since Victorian times. A beautiful walk begins here along Loch Etive (**walk 13d**).

The B845 which connects the Ardchattan road to Barcaldine is scenically marred by monotonous forestry plantations, although there is a grand view from the head of the pass towards Taynuilt and the hills of Lorn.

The main road heading north from Connel passes an airfield, where it is possible to arrange short glider flights. Benderloch village is dominated by the afforested slopes of **Beinn Lora** (**walk 9**). At the far end of the village, a minor road turns left to the Eriska Hotel. A mile along at **Tralee,** there is a rally carting track and one of the few and finest of the sandy beaches in the North Lorn area. At its southern end, a grassy hillock bears faint traces of an ancient Pictish fort. North of Tralee is the 16th century tower of **Barcaldine Castle.** Internally it has been modernised but still retains the old bottle neck dungeon and banqueting hall and claims to have a resident ghost (*daily May – Sept*).

Off the A828, beside beautiful Loch Creran is Argyll Pottery. Next door, the excellent **Sea Life Centre**, entertains both children and adults alike. Huge tanks recreate natural environments and house a great variety of fascinating marine life (*weekends in winter, daily March – Nov*).

Two miles on, just beyond the scattered housing and Kelco seaweed processing factory at Barcaldine, Victorian Douglas firs cluster around **Sutherland's Grove** car park and picnic place, from which leads excellent, easy forest walks (**walk 10**). Trout fishing is also available on the Glen Dubh Reservoir (tel: Mrs Lyon 01631 720469 regarding permits).

The road passes beneath a disused railway bridge spanning the narrows of Loch Creran which were created by glacial outwash deposits. Plans to transform the grandiose structure into a road bridge have been shelved for the time being. Instead one has to follow the twisting road for 6 miles around the impressive head of the loch, dominated by Creach Bheinn (**walk 10**) and a pair of fine Munros. Beyond the bridge over the River Creran, a minor road turns up Glen Creran, from which a walk leads northward to Ballachulish. Much of the early route is lined with monotonous conifers and views are severely restricted for 4 miles until the head of the pass. The east bank of the River Creran offers an easier and more pleasant alternative (end **walk 10**). Another track leading off from Glen Creran car park leads to Glen Ure. Colin Campbell lived in a house in the glen, the victim of the Appin Murder, made famous in Robert Louis Stephenson's, 'Kidnapped'. James Stewart was hung for the offence he did not commit. His memorial lies near Ballachulish Bridge to the north.

Approaching Appin, a single track road branches off at Inverfolla for North Shian and winds awkwardly through deciduous woodland with charming views to Loch Creran and the Isle of Eriska. From **Port Appin** a passenger ferry runs to Lismore. The harbour setting is enchanting in fine weather, especially when viewed at sunset. An easy walk south along the coast from the harbour car park affords fine views of Lismore and the Lynn of Lorn. Heading along the coast to Appin village, **Castle Stalker** is seen across Loch Laich perched on a tiny rocky island. The 13th century four storey tower, creates a dramatic picture at the mouth of the shallow loch, looking out to the hills of Morvern. Now in private hands, it is rarely open to the public.

LOCH LINNHE, GLENCOE & GLEN ETIVE

Having rejoined the A828 at Appin, the road now swings towards the shores of Loch Linnhe. At Lettershuna, Linnhe Marine Centre (*May-Sept*) teaches sailing and windsurfing. Clay pigeon shooting and pony trekking are also available. Throughout the next 6 miles, there are brief glimpses through a thin belt of trees across the loch to Ardgour whilst to your right, the heavily afforested Appin hills plunge steeply to the loch. To really appreciate the panoramic vistas one has to stop the car and walk. Just south of the hamlet of Duror, a left fork leads to Cuil and several short, very scenic routes (**walk 14**).

The road heads temporarily inland before meeting the sea once more at the tiny picturesque anchorage of Kentallon Bay. Garbh Bheinn forms a dramatic backcloth, seen across Loch Linnhe as you swing east under the equally impressive ramparts of Beinn a' Bheithir (**walk 15**). The direct route to Fort William now crosses the suspension bridge at the mouth of Loch Leven but this misses the many scenic delights to the east. The A82 is the much improved fast road to Crianlarich and the south. It bypasses the next village of **Ballachulish** which affords a number of tourist facilities (Tourist Information Centre *April – Oct*). The village was an important slate producer between 1690 and 1955, until cheaper imports signalled the industry's death knell. A teashop and craftshop now occupy some of the former slate workers' homes. The picturesque tiny harbour was created out of quarry waste material. Thanks to tree replanting and spoil shifting, little evidence remains of the quarries. Beside the loch, Highland Mystery World uses actors and animated effects to bring ancient Highland myths and legends to life. At the adjacent hotel, the small swimming pool and fitness room are open to non residents (also children's play area and short beautiful lochside walks).

The stately conical peak of the Pap of Glencoe, dominates the approach to Glencoe. A road forks left to **Glencoe Village.** The interesting folk museum is open May to September (*Mon – Sat*). Nearby some beautiful short walks have been laid out round the hospital lochan (see end **walk 16**). At the north east end of the village, a stone memorial cross stands in sad testament to the infamous Massacre of Glencoe, following the Macdonald's late oath of allegiance to King William III in 1692. Using this as an excuse, the Campbells settled some long standing scores and slew some 40 of the Macdonalds after having enjoyed their hospitality for two weeks. The Clachaig Inn 2 miles up the old road is a popular gathering place for the rock climbing fraternity and welcomes patrons with the sign, 'No credit, no Campbells.' Many clothing shops throughout Argyll still refuse to sell the Campbell tartan to avoid offence.

On the new road 2 miles south east of Glencoe village, a National Trust Centre provides an interesting insight into the history of local mountaineering and expounds on the massacre and local walks. Fishing permits for Loch Achtriochtan also available. From the centre there is an easy walk through the forest to Signal Rock, used by the Macdonald chiefs to summon their clansmen in times of emergency.

The road now enters the portals of the **Pass of Glencoe,** an awesome rock spectacular on either side. You will either be intimidated or excited;

this most dramatic of glens cannot fail to arouse the emotions. To the north, the Aonach Eagach ridge forms a continuous precipitous wall of cliffs and scree riven by gullies and topped by a succession of jagged pinnacles and peaks (**walk 16**). To the south, the truncated spurs of the 'Three Sisters' plunge in great broken cliffs, harbouring secretive hanging valleys. They dwarf the boisterous River Coe and its numerous tributaries which perform aquatic spectaculars when in spate. Particularly attractive are the Falls of Coe close to the junction of the A82 and the old road to Glencoe village. Further up the pass, a twin fall cascades over 60 feet in the 'Meeting of the Three Waters.' *All mountains should be treated with respect but for the Glencoe peaks this is doubly true.* Neither suitable for novice walkers nor bad weather ascents. For those fit enough to meet the challenge, Glencoe is a climbers and walkers mecca. National Trust Rangers arrange guided walks from their centre; particularly useful for the inexperienced.

Beyond the pass, the Glencoe ski area offers 15 runs for all abilities. One of the 6 lifts is open all year round allowing for aerial views of lonely bleak Rannoch Moor, a vast moorland with seemingly infinite lochans and boggy hollows, bordered by a clutch of fine Munros. Across the road from the ski area, the Kings House Hotel is reputedly the oldest inn in the country and a wonderful cosy port in a storm.

The A82 continues over the moor and descends to Bridge of Orchy where the B8074 turns off to follow the rumbustious River Orchy; another grand river when in spate and popular with salmon anglers. The Oban road is joined near Dalmally.

Returning to Kingshouse, a narrow winding road heads down into the relatively unspoilt **Glen Etive** to the head of Loch Etive, the 18 mile long sea loch we last met near Connel. Dominated by shapely Ben Starav (**walk 12**) and Beinn Trilleachan (**walk 13**), the loch is justifiably popular with walkers of all abilities and sea anglers; well worth the tortuous 13 mile drive from the main road. Connoisseurs of waterfalls could easily spend hours in the glen exploring a plethora of majestic falls. The finest are Eas an Fhir (grid reference 207513) on the River Etive, some 3.75 miles from the A82 junction; 0.75 mile on, Eas na Brogie (GR 191577) drops nearly 300 feet on a side stream tumbling through a chasm on the southern flanks of Buchaille Etive Mor; Dalness falls (GR 171511) where the Etive drops 20 feet in an impressive gorge (marked on the map just east of Dalness); Deirdrie's waterfall (GR161517) a three-tiered fall, half a mile west of Dalness on a small side stream in the forest; and the Robber's waterfall under Ben Starav (see **walk 13b**).

LOCH LEVEN TO FORT WILLIAM

For those heading north to Fort William from Glencoe, an alternative to the quick trip over the Ballachulish Bridge, is the 18 mile scenic drive around the fjord like Loch Leven, nestling under the great Mamore Forest mountains. Excellent walks abound in this area (see **walks 17, 18, 18a & 18b**). **Kinlochleven** at the head of the loch provides tourist accommodation, although is essentially a small industrial town which developed around the aluminium smelting works: being ideally sited for the production of hydro electric power and with easy access to the sea; an important consideration initially. A visitor centre in Linnhe Road (*April – Oct*) expounds on the history. Most houses are brightly painted in defence of the winter sunlight which cannot reach the town, owing to the close proximity of the mountains.

Rugged Garbh Bheinn, Glencoe and Beinn a' Bheithir create an impressive scene across the loch as one heads west along the north shore to rejoin the A82 at the small village of North Ballachulish. Here a sweet factory visitor centre is open all year. Beyond, the wild hills of Ardgour are seen majestically across Loch Linnhe. Tantalizing vistas to the west continue intermittently all the way to Fort William when breaks in the forest allow.

A mile north of Onich's line of hotels, a forest road bears left to Inchree and the Falls of Glenrigh (**walk 15a**), easily missed by the majority of rushing tourists. Closeby, the Corran vehicle ferry runs across the narrows of Loch Linnhe; another example of the deposition of glacial outwash.

FORT WILLIAM

Although not the prettiest of towns, its setting beside Loch Linnhe is glorious. The fort after which it is named, was originally built in 1655 and later improved. It was flattened in 1894 to make way for the railway. The Glasgow – Fort William line is one of the few Highland lines to survive economic cutbacks, though its future is not entirely certain. May to October, steam trains run to Mallaig along one of the most scenic rail lines in Europe.

Being a popular tourist centre, there is a large range of accommodation (Tourist Information Centre, Cameron Square *open all year*) and shops. The town is a great place for buying woollens and tweeds. Business has been greatly boosted by the **Aonach Mor** ski-ing development 7 miles to the north (18 runs at all levels and dry slope). A gondola lift runs throughout the summer months to a high restaurant, enabling none walkers to enjoy fine aerial vistas to the Great Glen and westward to the distant Hebrides. Several short easy to follow paths lead from the bottom car park and the top restaurant. Seal island cruises are available in summer (01397 705589) and Loch Eil and Loch Linnhe offer good sailing and sea fishing.

Wet weather escapes include the interesting **West Highland Museum** (*Mon – Sat*) in Cameron Square which houses natural history exhibits and historical relics from the Neolithic Age to the Jacobites. **Ben Nevis Distillery** on the A82 opposite the Mallaig road junction, has a small exhibition and shop. There is a golf course nearby and a leisure centre offers swimming, a gym, squash, climbing wall, table tennis and tennis.

The only fine building in town is **St Andrew's Episcopal Church,** built in pink granite, close to the confluence of the Water of Nevis and Loch Linnhe. Three quarters of a mile north of the Glen Nevis roundabout, a signed road leads left to the well preserved 13th century **Inverlochy Castle.** Four towers and 20 foot curtain walls remain. Closeby was the scene of a famous battle in 1645 when the Royalist Montrose heavily defeated the covenanting army under Campbell of Argyll. This inspite of being outnumbered two to one and having made one of the most arduous and daring route marches in British history to take Campbell by surprise. Across the main road is the aluminium works below the flanks of Ben Nevis, built at the end of the First World War. Somewhat of an eyesore, as with Kinlochleven, it is an important employer in an area where good jobs are hard to come by.

Just beyond the works, the road to Mallaig branches left and in a mile reaches the **Caledonian Canal** at Banavie. Fort William's development has been largely due to its superb position as a route centre with extensive road, rail and sea links with much of Scotland. It is a seaport although 20 miles from the open sea and is linked to the east coast by the Caledonian Canal combined with Lochs Ness, Oich and Lochy, which follow the Great Glen fault line. At Banavie, the 8 locks of Neptune's Staircase, raise the canal 80 feet. An excellent, easy walk follows the canal tow path for the 4 miles to Loch Lochy. Either return the same way or take the usually quiet B8004 road for grand views across the canal and river. Ben Nevis and its adjoining peaks are well seen along this route.

Ben Nevis, Britain's highest mountain, (see the end of **walk 20**) is a great tourist magnet. Although overlooking Fort William, the flanks of **Brown Cow Hill (walk 19)** hide it from the town itself. It is best seen from the north and west. In September there is a hill race from the town to its summit and back. Other annual events of note are the Highland Games, usually in *late July* and a large agricultural show in *August.*

Arguably the most beautiful glen in Scotland, the exploration of **Glen Nevis** to the immediate south east of the town, is a must for both walker and tourist alike. In the lower valley, the river and fields are flanked by Ben Nevis to the left and the afforested peaks of the Mamores to the right. Sgurr a' Mhaim and Stob Ban are impressive at the head of the first part of the glen. The **Ionad Nibheis Centre** explains about the areas flora and fauna (*March – Nov*). The road turns sharply east at the Falls of Polldubh. There is a car park just beyond the road bridge. The wide curtain falls, 40 feet in height, plunge spectacularly into a rocky gorge. Surrounded by birch trees and overlooked by the craggy mountains, it is a magical spot. The road now narrows considerably and in 2 miles reaches a car park; above which a 1250 foot water slide cascades down the grey slabs of Ben Nevis. Numerous fine walks begin here (see **walk 20**).

For those tourists wishing to escape the summer crowds of North Argyll and the Fort William area, you need only to cross on the Corran Ferry and enter the region of Ardgour. Combined with Morvern, Ardnamurchan and Moidart, they form a large empty quarter, sparsely populated, largely roadless and often ignored by visitors; being totally devoid of Munros. It is a land, however, rich in flora and fauna and with many beautiful corners and affording superb seascapes. Historically the area is important, being particularly associated with the wanderings of Bonnie Prince Charlie and early Christian worship. The only problem you will encounter when visiting here is that, with the exception of the regular bus and rail services running between Mallaig and Fort William, public transport is poor in the region and a car is desirable. But petrol stations are few and it is advisable to keep your car filled up.

CORPACH, LOCH EIL, ARDGOUR & MORVERN

Heading west from Fort William on the A830 road to Mallaig, you soon pass Corpach. Although largely industrial, it provides grand views across the confluence of Lochs Eil and Linnhe to Ben Nevis and is home to a gem of a tourist attraction – literally! The award winning **Treasures of the Earth** houses a stunning collection of gems, crystals and fossils in creative settings (*open daily Feb – Dec except Christmas*). In Gaelic, Corpach translates as the *place of the bodies*, because corpses of northern nobles were rested here en route for burial on Iona.

Gaps in the flanking trees allow fine views to the Lochaber mountains as you head westward along **Loch Eil.** Just beyond Kinlocheil, a much quieter road branches left and follows the delightful southern shore of the loch, with stands of deciduous woodland augmenting the views to the mountains. Beyond Loch Eil the road turns down Loch Linnhe and passes through Camusnagaul, connected to Fort William by passenger ferry. From Stronchreggan House an attractive narrow glen leads to an easy Corbett **Stob Coire a' Chearcaill (walk 32)**. Four miles on, the road skirts the shallow Inverscaddle Bay, which looks out to Ben Nevis and is overlooked by Conaglen House, a large sporting estate offering excellent fishing and stalking. Glen Scaddle and Glen Cona lead off to the west; opportunities for easy valley walks on good tracks. Beyond the bay, the roadsides are a blaze of colour in June from a proliferation of rhododendrons amidst the pines and larches. Corran with its regular ferry across Loch Linnhe, stands in the shadow of **Sgurr na h-Eanchainne** (walk 33). Just to the north at Cille Mhaodian, there was once a cell of a Celtic church dedicated to St Broden. Only the graveyard now remains, used as a burial place for the MacLeans of Ardgour since the 15th century.

At Inversanda the main road turns inland to Strontian along Glen Tarbert, flanked by mighty **Garbh Bheinn (walk 34)**. A narrow minor road continues along Loch Linnhe to picturesque **Kingairloch (walk 35)** then heads inland to join the A884. When the weather is too poor to allow proper appreciation of the loch, a superb series of rivers, gorges and falls will more than compensate. Turning south to Lochaline, bleak moorland gives way to wooded Gleann Geal with an attractive river offering good fishing. At the foot of the glen, an easy track leads north from Acharn into a wildlife reserve (**walk 36**).

A mile south, a minor road bears right to Kinloch. The south side of **Loch Arienas** is heavily planted with confers through which two cycle routes of 5.5km and 14.5km have been laid out. By contrast the north shore is home to enchanting native woodland (**walk 36**). From **Kinloch** above Loch Teacuis, there is a variety of walking amidst charming surroundings, rich in wildlife (**walk 37**).

The main road winds south into the delightful wooded strath of the River Aline. The minor road for Ardtornish leads to the head of Loch Aline and the partially restored 15th century square keep of **Kinlochaline Castle** standing on a small crag in a beautiful setting.

This was locally known as the *castle of butter*, since the labourers who built it were allegedly paid in butter rather than cash. Originally the seat of Clan MacInnes, it passed into the hands of Maclean of Duart before being burnt during the Civil War. On the east side of the River Aline, the Victorian **Ardtornish House** is surrounded by a 28 acre garden with woodland walks (*open April – Oct*). Fishing for salmon, brown trout and sea trout is also available. Nearby, a rough road runs down to the ruins of the 14th century **Ardtornish Castle (walk 38)**.

From **Lochaline,** there are views across to Mull and along the Sound of Mull and past Duart Castle to the Lorn coast, particularly from outside the Church of St Columba above the village. Although not built till 1898, in the grounds lie remains of a medieval chapel and a nine foot tall, 15th century Celtic cross. Apart from a diving school, boat hire for sea fishing and a regular vehicle ferry to Mull, there is little else here. Aesthetically, the village has been spoilt by local timber felling and the important mine which produces pure silicon sand for optical glass.

The narrow but scenic B849 initially runs high above the Sound of

Mull before passing through some attractive deciduous stands and dropping to a rocky coast with excellent views to the high hills of Mull. A Site of Special Scientific Interest allows no public access but orchids, rare ferns and a multitude of other plants can be found near the roadside. Ornithologists can enjoy a great variety of birds. Buzzards in particular are often seen at very close quarters. The area suffered badly during the Highland Clearances and the highway passes a number of deserted townships. Beyond Finnary, a curious archway lies next to the road. A result of the sea having eroded through a volcanic dyke before the water receded. To the west stands the remains of Casteal nan Con, *'the castle of hounds'*, a former hunting lodge for the Lords of the Isles. Its fish trap can still be seen at low tide. The road ends in 11 miles at **Drimnin**, from where a scenic track rises gently above the Sound of Mull to the ruined houses of Auliston (see **walk 39**).

Unless crossing to Mull, it is now necessary to backtrack along the A884 to Loch Sunart. At Liddesdale a twisting narrow road turns off to **Laudale** with great views of the loch en route and from the track beyond (**walk 40**).

Turning west onto the A861, you soon reach **Strontian,** a village with good tourist facilities (including a Tourist Information Centre *April – Oct* and craft workshops) which developed around the local mines, and the discovery in 1764 of a metallic element now known as strontium. Strontian was also famed for its floating church which was anchored nearby in 1843. The local Laird refused to let members of the Free Presbyterian Church have their own chapel so they purchased an old boat and converted it into a church, which was towed to Loch Sunart from Glasgow.

One mile north of the village, a signposted nature trail near Scotstown (**walk 41A**) leads through pretty native woodland to some old lead mines. The steep narrow road ends at Polloch by beautiful Loch Shiel, dominated in the south by craggy **Beinn Resipol** (**walk 41**). From the road end one can walk or cycle along the gentle well surfaced private road running northward up the eastern shore. Alternatively one can follow an old coffin road from Polloch westward to Achnanellan. The burial ground lies on the tiny islet of Eilean Fhianain, named after St Finian who built a sanctuary there in the 6th century. His bronze bell remains and is believed to posses the power of healing.

The main road winds westward through attractive stands of oak and birch fringing pretty Loch Sunart, the haunt of otters and seals. Five miles west of Strontian the Forestry Commission has laid out an easy walk amongst mixed woodland which includes wonderful views of the loch. Popular with anglers and yachtsmen, its waters are not suitable for novices and require local knowledge. The road passes through the small village of

Salen which grew up round its attractive harbour and a textile mill of which nothing remains. Above the busy yacht haven on the east side of the village, there is a car park and waymarked mile long walk through oak-wood with rare plants and views over the bay.

ARDNAMURCHAN

The road divides at Salen, north to Moidart or westward for 17 miles along the Ardnamurchan Peninsula. The latter passes through Laga where one can hire boats (tel 01972 500208) for fishing and wildlife cruises on Loch Sunart. World War II convoys assembled on the loch and the nearby Edwardian Glenborrodale 'Castle' became a temporary naval base. The castellated towers of this imposing edifice can be glimpsed through the huge clusters of roadside rhododendrons. Sheltering the bay, small off-shore islands provide breeding grounds for many ducks and wading birds. Two miles on is the award-winning **Ardnamurchan Natural History Centre** where there is an excellent audio visual show and cameras provide live coverage at feeding tables and in underwater pools (*April-Oct*).

In a further 2 miles, a car park stands above the beautiful small bay of **Camas na Geal (walk 42)**. Here the red carved stone of Cladh Chiarain was possibly dedicated by St Columba, a monument to the 6th century Irish Saint, Ciaran. There is also an even earlier standing stone, which has a carving of a cross and a dog on it.

The road now turns inland and climbs over rather bleak moorland passing beneath imposing **Beinn Hiant (walk 43)**, a grand viewpoint. The hilly hinterland is mostly uncultivated. A few scattered crofts survive on the coastal fringes where the ice-scoured rocky ground has been fertilised by wind blown calcareous sand. Rare birds abound and wild flowers flourish on the machair, seen at their best from *late May through July*. The road returns briefly to the sea at **Kilchoan**, an attractive crofting village standing in a wide bay with safe secluded beaches, looking out to the mountains of Movern and Mull. There is a Tourist Information Centre (*April – Oct*) and a vehicle ferry to Tobermory (*passenger only in winter*). Above the settlement is a ruined 18th church which incorporated an earlier 12th century chapel. Near Kilchoan lies the 13th century **Mingary Castle**, a stronghold of the MacIains of Ardnamurchan for some 400 years. It stands in a grand cliff top setting guarding the entrance to the Sound of Mull. Although well preserved, unfortunately it is unsafe to explore too closely. It lies along a private road but can be reached by following a signed path round fields and shingle shoreline from a car park off the B8007 just east of Kilchoan.

Beyond Kilchoan, the road divides. Taking the right fork gains the hamlet of Sanna. **Sanna Bay** is actually four bays of white shell sand split by rocky points, which make good fishing stances. The sand dunes are backed by flower filled machair pasture. Several short walks are possible from here (**walk 44**) with fine views to the Western Isles.

The left fork leads across moorland to the *Point of the Great Ocean,* **Ardnamurchan Point**, the most westerly point on mainland Britain. The lighthouse, built in 1849, stands on a low, storm battered cliff looking to Coll, Muck, Tiree, Rum, Mull and the Outer Hebrides; a splendid place on a clear day. A Visitor Centre expounds on the history of lighthouse keeping and the natural history of the area. With patience, otters and seals can be seen along this rocky and fretted coast. It is also another area popular with botanists.

Returning eastwards, a minor road bears left to Kilmory passing over open farming land nestling between rocky outcrops. The grasslands above the sea are another botanical paradise. One-and-a-half miles along this road, a road branches left for Fascadale following Achateny Water. One mile along, at Achateny, one can walk along a track which crosses the river and passes the houses to reach a flat sandy bay with rocky wave cut platforms. The views to the Inner Hebrides are superb. Continuing along the main road to **Kilmory**, another fine beach can be reached on foot. Park 200 yards beyond Kilmory Post Office and take the easy track to the sea. The road ends at **Ockle** from where a track heads eastward above the coast to Kentra Bay, affording grand vistas to seaward and Moidart (**walk 45**)

MOIDART

North of Salen, **Acharacle** is an attractive small crofting village and tourist centre which once boasted a population of more than 2000 before being dcimated by the 19th century clearances. It is a great base for walking, fishing, canoeing, pony trekking and sailing (boat hire available). At the end of the village, a narrow road turns off to the popular small picturesque sandy coves around **Ardtoe**, from where a short ascent leads to the summit of Carn Mor (**walk 46**). A branch road bears left towards the south shore of the shallow and attractive Kentra Bay, surrounded by innumerable rocky hills. At Arivegaig there is parking through a gate, beyond which begins the long, but easy, aforementioned track to Ockle.

Soon after crossing the impressive arched stone bridge spanning the River Shiel to the north of Acharacle, a road bears off left to Dorlin on Loch Moidart. Here at low tide one can cross the sandy causeway to reach the 14th century **Castle Tioram**, built on a rocky promontory (**walk 47**).

A mile beyond Shiel Bridge, the main road passes through Mingarry where in summer you can visit the 'Illegal Museum', which tells of old illegal poaching and distiling practices. It is housed in athatched 'black house', which was typical of crofters homes until the 20th century.

The road now climbs over moorland to reach the head of Loch Moidart. A minor road continues eastward for 2 miles into pretty Glen Moidart (**walk 49A**). The main road follows the north shore of the loch past old Kinlochmoidart House where Bonnie Prince Charlie waited for a week whilst rallying initial support. It was subsequently destroyed by Cumberland's troops after Culloden. From the pier at nearby Dalelia, the Prince was rowed up Loch Shiel to Glenfinnan, where he raised his standard. By the side of Loch Moidart, seven trees stand in memorial to the seven loyal followers who accompanied the Prince from France.

Beyond another moorland pass the road drops to Glenuig, from where a narrow lane branches west past a traditional inn, parts of which date back two centuries. From the road-end an easy attractive walk leads to Smirisary (**walk 48**). The main road continues along Loch Ailort, a corruption from the Norse, All-fjord, 'deep fjord'. A vitrified fort stands at its mouth on Eilean nan Gobhar, one of four in the area which guarded the sea approaches from Ardnamurchan. Overlooking the loch, **Rois-Bheinn** is a superb viewpoint (**walk 49**)

Near the head of the loch, the imposing building of Inverailort Castle was used as a training base for 42 Commando during World War II, an indication of the roughness of terrain hereabouts. Further east at Arisaig House, the Special Operations Executive trained resistance agents.

Turning left at Lochailort, the A830 Mallaig road heads westward to **Loch nan Uamh**. Here Bonnie Prince Charlie landed from Eriskay at the start of his campaign in July 1745. He departed for France in September 1746 after his long and harrowing escape from Culloden. A cairn lies here as a poignant reminder. On a clear day, the attractive bay looks out to the Isles of Rum and Eigg. The loch is overlooked by the craggy small hill of Cruach an Fhearainn Duibh, a superb viewpoint, reached by a short hill-walk from Polnish, a mile to the east (**walk 50**). A mile beyond the Prince's cairn, the Beasdale Burn flows under the road. The falls along its course provide an attractive destination when the weather is unkind (**walk 51**).

The road briefly leaves the coast to cross a beautifully wooded and rhododendron bedecked peninsula, rejoining the sea at the small village of **Arisaig**, a yachting and tourist centre dominated by its church tower. Its clock is a memorial to the revered Gaelic poet Alistair MacMhaighstir Alasdair, who fought with the Jacobites at Culloden. The houses stand in a rocky bay with impressive views to the Hebrides. In summer Murdo Grant runs popular cruises to the Small Isles (tel: 01687 546224). The more energetic can hire cycles in the village. Heading westward out of Arisaig, a single track road along the headland leads to a small seal colony near Rhumach. The scenic road is usually quiet and best enjoyed by walking.

The main road now heads north through a barer landscape, passing the picturesquely sited 9-hole golf course at Traigh and numerous sandy bays and coves. Five miles north of Arisaig there is a large car park just beyond Glenancross House, from where a short path leads down to the sandy beach backed by dunes. The heather and crag clad hill of Beinn an Achaidh Mhoir overlooks the north side of the bay. Although only 88m/ 289ft high, it is a breathtaking viewpoint for the Western Isles, Moidart coast and beautiful Loch Morar. At sunset, the vistas are simply stunning. If you never climb another hill again, do try and ascend this one! Access can be gained just around the crown of a bend in the road, 200 yards uphill of the car park. Grassy corridors weave easily if steeply between the outcrops – you can gain the trig point in 10 – 15 minutes.

Two miles on lie the famed dazzling silver sands of **Morar**. Although popular with film directors ('Rob Roy', 'Highlander' and 'Local Hero' were partly filmed hereabouts) and with summer holiday-makers, a short walk can secure you a quiet, secluded cove with enchanting views to the islands. A few yards south of Morar railway station, a set of steps lead up to a metal cross erected in 1899 to commemorate the opening of the present church. Unlike the ugly cross, the views are beautiful over Loch Morar and seaward to Rum. Loch Morar is the deepest inland loch in Europe, although its short outflow debauches into a very shallow sea. Over a thousand feet deep, its trench owes its origins to a geological fault. Legend tells of its own less well publicised monster, Morag, to rival Nessie. There is plenty of great fishing on the loch for lesser fry. Energetic anglers can also enjoy good trout fishing in the hill lochs to the north, including Loch 'an Nostarie and Loch Eiregoraidh. A scenic minor road follows the north shore of **Loch Morar** for 4 miles to Bracorina from where several fine walks begin (**walk 52**).

The road ends at the bustling fishing port and ferry terminal of **Mallaig**. Although not attractive in itself, there are fine views from the harbour and its environs and playful seals often swim close to shore. Vehicle ferries run to Skye, Barra and South Uist whilst passenger services serve Muck, Rum, Canna, Inverie in Knoydart, Tarbert and Kyle of Lochalsh. Further details can be obtained from the Tourist Information Centre (*April – Oct*). **Mallaig Marine World** near the harbour (*open all year*) houses tanks of sea creatures and an exhibition which tells of the town's fishing tradition. **The Heritage Centre** in Stanon Road expounds on local history and includes an exhibition of old photos of Mallaig and its surrounds (*Easter – Nov*). For a relatively easy stroll with superb views try the trail to Mallaigmore. Hill-walkers can continue onto the rough hills to the east (**walk 53**).

Unless taking a ferry, one must now return along the Fort William road. A mile-and-a-half east of Lochailort, a path leaves the roadside and crosses the wild South Morar peninsula to reach Camas Luinge Bay on Loch Morar (**walk 54A**). The scenic drive eastward past Loch Eilt culminates at **Glenfinnan** with a superb view down Loch Shiel, dominated on the left by **Sgurr Ghuibhsachain** (**walk 56**). Here Bonnie Prince Charlie raised his standard on 19 August 1745, proclaiming his exiled father King James III and VIII of Scotland, changing the history of the Highlands forever. The striking monument to the clansmen, with its statue of a Highlander, was erected by a descendant of the Prince in 1815. Unfortunately this monument may have to close owing to dangerous subsidence. The adjacent National Trust Visitor Centre relates the story of the Prince's doomed campaign (*daily April – Oct*). A beautifully situated Catholic Church standing above the loch contains another monument to the Prince. To fully appreciate unspoilt Loch Shiel try a walk along the traffic free eastern shore (see the end of **walk 56**) or take a short pleasure cruise (*April to October*). The pier is popular with anglers. Annually, in August, a popular Highland games is held in the grounds surrounding the monument. A few hundred yards to the north lies a magnificent curving railway viaduct designed by Sir Robert 'Concrete Bob' McAlpine. A railway museum at Glenfinnan Station tells of the scenic West Highland Line (*daily June – Sept, more limited opening other months*). A classic Munro walk starts here (**walk 55**) and from 2 miles to the west, a fine rocky Corbett can be ascended (**walk 54**).

WALKING SECTIONS – EXPLANATORY NOTES

The walks are described in detail (unless the route is waymarked and obvious) and supported by accompanying maps where necessary. For the hill-walkers, the maps in the book are for illustrative purposes and are not intended to make the use of an Ordnance Survey map redundant. Heights reached in each walk are shown in both feet (ft) and metres (m) as most of us still think imperially, although the maps are now metric.

Gaelic is not an easy language to pronounce. To help you pronounce the hill you are climbing, a phonetic pronunciation is given in brackets after most mountain names. This can only be an approximation however, given that a number of Gaelic sounds are totally foreign to English, some names have been corrupted and regional variations in pronounciation exist.

Each major walk has an accompanying **FACT FILE** showing:

Total distance of the walk in miles.

Where the walk involves some climbing, the amount of **height gain** is shown both in feet & metres.

The **time** given is an average time, including stops, in good summer conditions. Time taken may be *much longer* in adverse conditions or if terrain is snow covered.

The **start** and **finish** points are given along with an **OS Sheet num ber.** This is for the relevant Ordnance Survey 1 50,000 sheet for that area, the most frequently used scale by walkers. All OS maps are drawn on a numbered grid of kilometre squares and 6 figure grid references (GR) are used.

The **remarks** section highlights any potential difficulties of terrain under certain conditions.

Stalking season refers to any restriction during the deer stalking season. Stags are culled *1 July – 20 October* and hinds *21 October – 15 February.* Usually estates will allow access to the hills if no shooting is taking place. They often post local notices at access points regarding shooting but these may be missed, especially if you are an early riser. Estate contact phone numbers have been given where available. The onus is on the walker to check first. Tourist offices can also assist. The most critical time to check on access is from *mid-August to mid-October,* (this also includes the most critical time for grouse shooting). Most of the land is under private ownership and walkers who are considered trespassers can be required to leave that land. Reasonable force may be used to remove them. Freedom to roam the hills relies on the traditional mutual tolerance between landowners and the public. It is essential that walkers respect the necessary activities of the estates and do not interrupt the shooting. It should also be noted that it is an offence to camp or light fires on private land without the consent of the landowner. The estate contact numbers can be used to obtain such permission.

Dog owners should note that it is imperative to keep your dog under very close control at all times and on a lead when anywhere near sheep. During the **lambing period** (*April/May*), estates request that dogs are not taken through fields of sheep. Remember, a landowner is legally entitled to shoot any dog which is a threat to livestock.

Public transport if available is noted, including post buses. Tourist Information Centres can assist with timetables. Many of the walks, but not all, can be reached by limited public transport, and a private car is by far the most convenient mode of transport in the Highlands. Any likely parking problems are mentioned in the text of the walk. Please ensure that you do not block narrow roads, bearing in mind that farm vehicles and vehicles as large as Calor Gas tankers need to get through on the most minor of roads.

The Walks

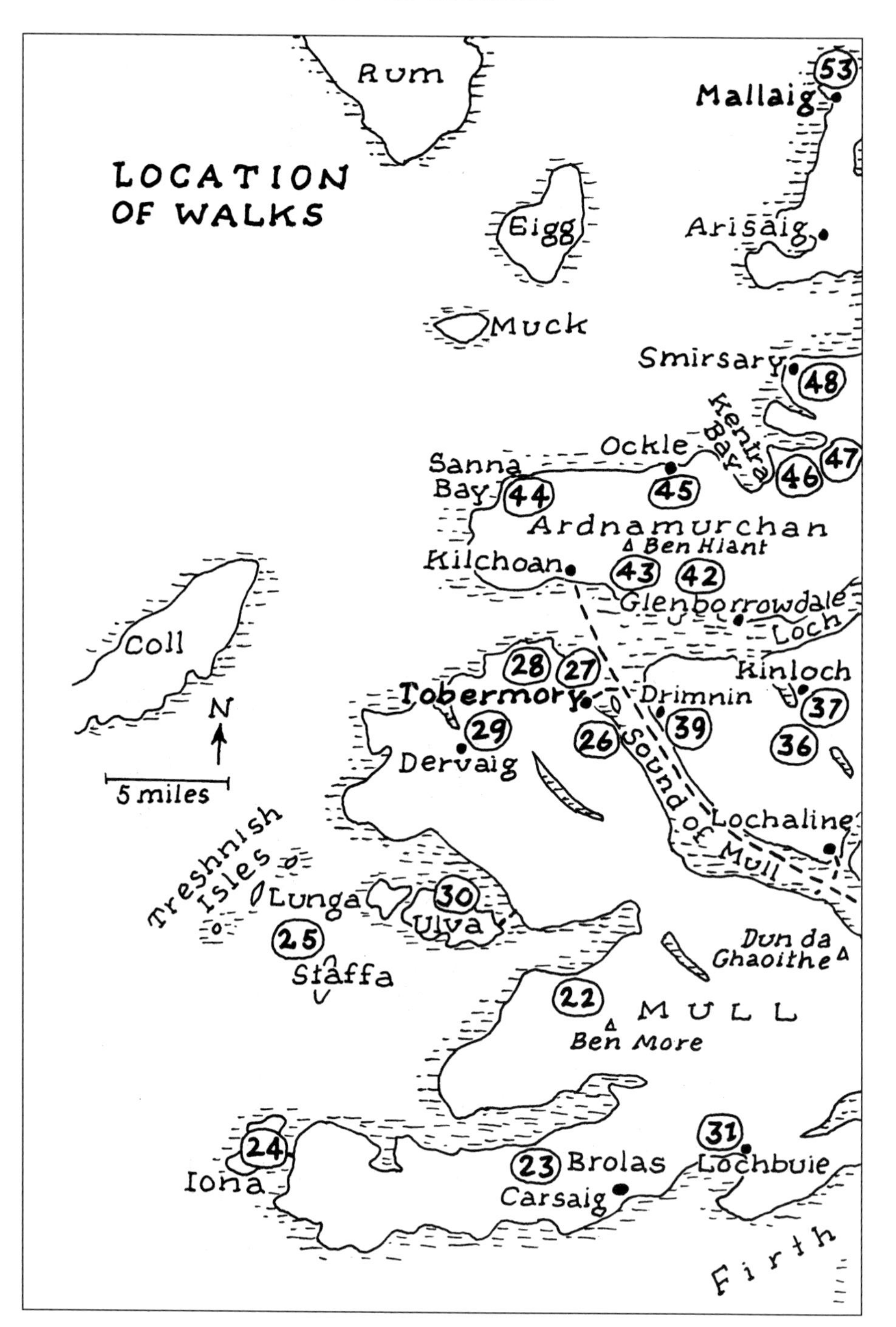
LOCATION OF WALKS
Rum
Mallaig
53
Eigg
Arisaig
Muck
Smirsary
48
Kentra Bay
Ockle
47
46
Sanna Bay
44
45
Ardnamurchan
Ben Hiant
Kilchoan
43
42
Glenborrowdale
Loch
Coll
28
27
Kinloch
Tobermory
Drimnin
37
N
29
26
39
36
Dervaig
Sound of Mull
5 miles
Treshnish Isles
Lochaline
Lunga
30
Ulva
25
Staffa
Dun da Ghaoithe
22
MULL
Ben More
31
24
23
Brolas
Lochbuie
Iona
Carsaig
Firth

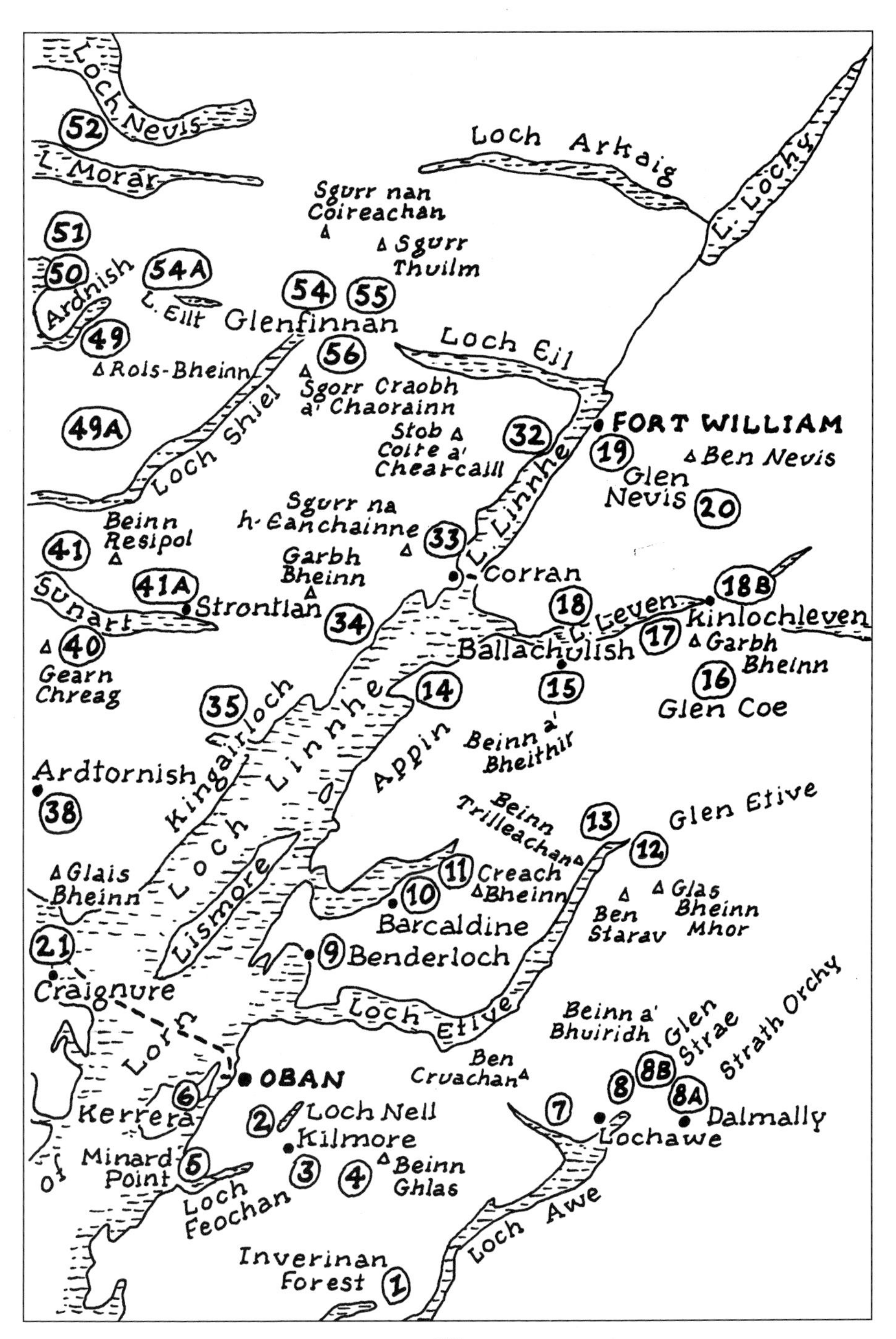
Loch Nevis
52
L. Morar
Loch Arkaig
L. Lochy
Sgurr nan Coireachan
Sgurr Thuilm
51
50
Ardnish
54A
L. Eilt
54
55
Glenfinnan
Loch Eil
49
56
Rois-Bheinn
Sgorr Craobh a' Chaorainn
Loch Shiel
49A
Stob Coire a' Chearcaill
32
L. Linnhe
FORT WILLIAM
19
Ben Nevis
Glen Nevis
20
Sgurr na h-Eanchainne
Beinn Resipol
41
33
Garbh Bheinn
Corran
41A
Sunart
Strontian
34
18
18B
L. Leven
Kinlochleven
17
Garbh Bheinn
40
Ballachulish
Gearn Chreag
14
15
16
Glen Coe
35
Kingairloch
Loch Linnhe
Appin
Beinn a' Bheithir
Ardtornish
38
Beinn Trilleachan
13
Glen Etive
12
Glais Bheinn
Loch
Lismore
11
Creach Bheinn
10
Glas Bheinn Mhor
Ben Starav
Barcaldine
21
9
Benderloch
Craignure
Loch Etive
Beinn a' Bhuiridh
Glen Strae
Strath Orchy
Lorn
Ben Cruachan
OBAN
6
8
8B
7
8A
Kerrera
2
Loch Nell
Dalmally
Lochawe
Kilmore
Minard Point
5
3
4
Beinn Ghlas
of
Loch Feochan
Loch Awe
Inverinan Forest
1

1 INVERLIEVER FOREST WALKS

A question with which to fool your friends. How long does it take without flying to reach New York? The answer if you're staying in or around Oban, is less than an hour. Scotland has its very own 'Big Apple' on the western shore of Loch Awe. It lies in an attractive area of low hills and intimate small lochans and bristles with easy to follow gentle forest walks, which make for very pleasant and easy outings when the weather is too inclement for the hills.

At Kilmelford, 14 miles south of Oban on the A816, a scenic narrow road, turns east and runs along Loch Avich to the small forestry village of Dalavich. From here, a path follows the shore of Lochawe southward and in less than a mile reaches New York, which today is little more than a ruined house and pier. It

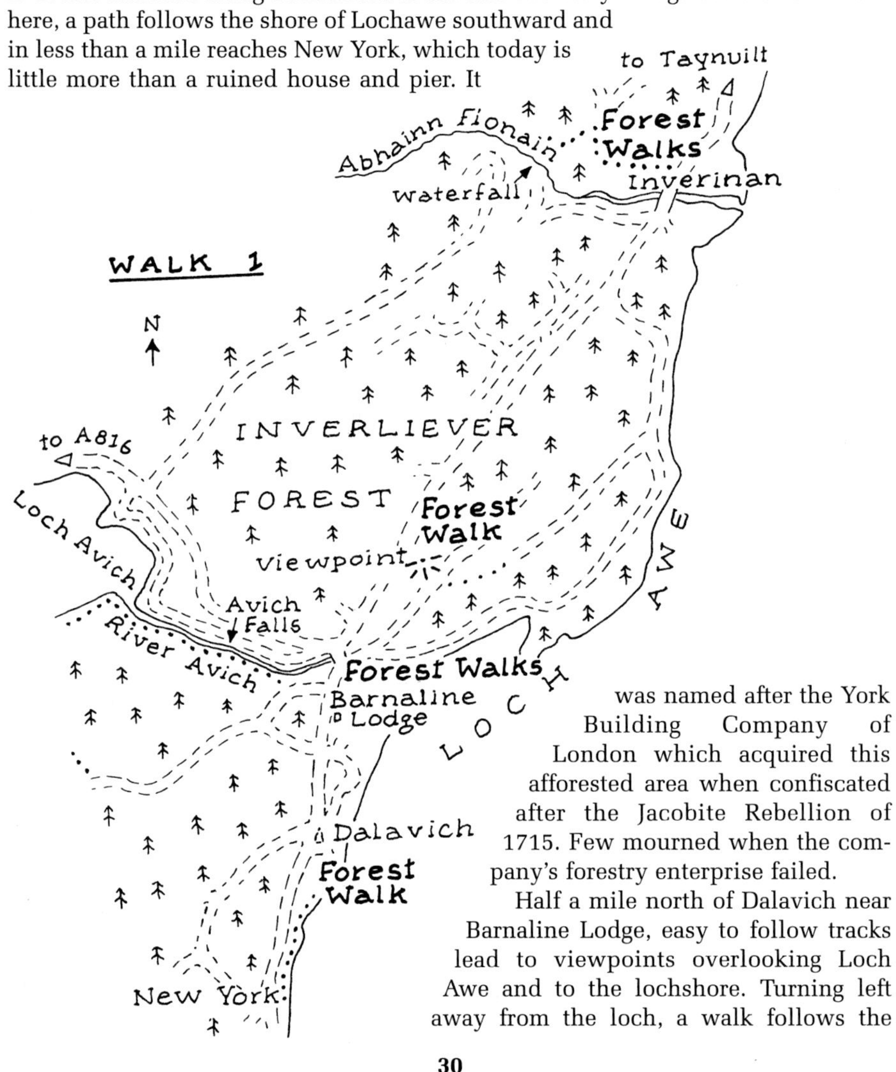

was named after the York Building Company of London which acquired this afforested area when confiscated after the Jacobite Rebellion of 1715. Few mourned when the company's forestry enterprise failed.

Half a mile north of Dalavich near Barnaline Lodge, easy to follow tracks lead to viewpoints overlooking Loch Awe and to the lochshore. Turning left away from the loch, a walk follows the banks of the River Avich which tumbles in a number of beautiful waterfalls. Beyond the falls, a track on the north bank continues easily for a further 1.5 miles along the eastern end of Loch Avich. Many oak trees mingle with the conifers and at quiet times of day you may be lucky enough to spy roe and red deer and a variety of birds of prey.

From Inverinan some 3 miles north of Dalavich, a waymarked walk through attractive deciduous woodland, leads in about 30 minutes to a bridge over a picturesque waterfall on the Abhainn Fionain.
(Public transport: poor bus service Oban to Dalavich via Taynuilt; only allows 1 hour at Dalavich and 1.5 hours at Inverinan)

2 THE GREAT WEE HILLS OF KILMORE

Five miles south of Oban, a series of small, rough, grassy hills rise steeply above the bungalows of the Barran Estate near Kilmore. Little known except to locals, they provide superb viewpoints despite their lowly height; the highest being Sron Mhor 198m/650ft. When I used to live at Barran, this rewarding walk was my favourite short hill circuit and was the one I missed most after leaving. In addition to the scenic splendours, there is usually plenty of avian interest.

Park near the Water Board building close to the south west corner of enchanting Loch Nell on the Kilmore to Connel road. Follow the quiet road south towards Kilmore. Keep an eye open for the swans which nest each year on the tiny islet at this end of the loch. Otters too occasionally frequent these waters. The road meets the River Nell, the haunt of grey herons. Stonechats and kestrels often patrol the fields beside the road. A quarter of a mile from the loch, bear left over the river bridge at Barnacarry and follow the track towards the farm. Fork right at a track junction just before the buildings and go through a metal gate. Turn right and immediately take the narrow sheep track following the base of the hill southward, just above the wall and fence. Cross the burn and continue to follow the hill through rough sheep grazing land, keeping approximately midway between the Barran houses on your right and a dilapidated wall to the left. A short way on, a small but lively burn splits Sron Mhor from a nameless hill to the left. Follow the left bank upstream passing a small waterfall. A distinct sheep track starts here and cuts up to the left across the face of the scree riddled hill. Ignore this and keep on uphill, taking a less obvious path up the crest of the small ridge. Towards the top, keep to the right side of the hill and gradually descend to the small defile under Sron Mhor, making full use of the sheep tracks on the steep rocky slopes. From the dip, slant up right on steep grassy ground to reach a fence below some coniferous plantings. Follow the fence along to the right hand corner. Climb over with care then yomp up through the heather to the summit of Sron Mhor, weaving between the thinly scattered trees. Buzzards nest near here and are regularly seen circling above. The absorbing panoramic views extend to all the high hills of Mull, the Sound of Mull, the mountains half way up Loch Linnhe, Loch Feochan and eastward to Ben Cruachan.

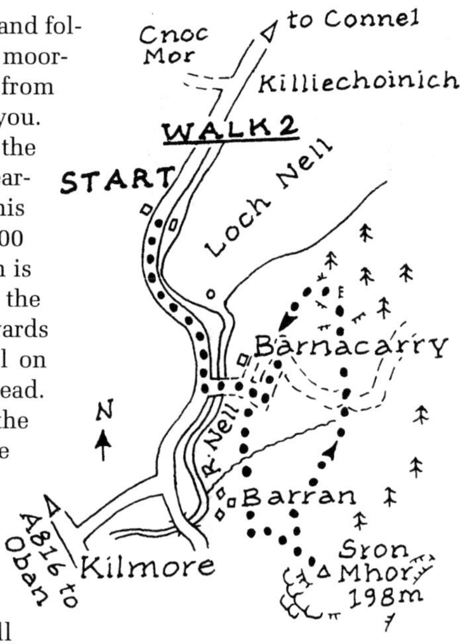

Retrace your steps to the small defile and follow this up beside the burn. Open rough moorland is reached with the track from Barnacarry some 400 yards ahead of you. The next target is the highest ground to the immediate left of the track (compass bearing approximately 6 degrees). Aim for this little hill, crossing the track some 100 yards below a prominent waterfall which is very attractive after heavy rain. From the hilltop, keep straight on and in 200 yards gain the top of another grassy rise. Still on the same bearing, the last summit lies ahead. To reach its base, descend slightly to the right to avoid the steepest ground. The hill is a grand viewpoint overlooking all of Loch Nell.

Descend the west ridge for 50 yards to the foot of a small grassy knoll. Turn down to the right and follow the base of this knoll round to a small craggy dip with the Barran estate and the River Nell seen beyond. Continue straight on, down a wide grassy gully for about 100 yards then bear slightly left onto a sheep track which easily crosses two burns to gain the track just above Barnacarry. Rejoin your outward route just beyond the farm.

For those staying in the Oban area and desirous of a longer walk, then take the bus to Kilmore rather than drive. Having completed the above walk, continue along the Connel road climbing above Loch Nell, passing through delightful oak woodland. On reaching Killiechoinich Farm, turn left up a good track which climbs gently below Cnoc Mor hill (the summit is another fine viewpoint and worth a short detour) before entering a forest. Half a mile into the trees, fork right at a track junction and in another half mile turn left. On reaching the road, bear left and head down into Oban past the golf course.

FACT FILE

Distance: 3.5 miles Height gain 800 ft/ 244m (Oban alternative 6.5 miles; 1100ft / 335m)

Time: 1.5 – 2 hours

Start/ Finish: Loch Nell GR 883227 OS Sheet 49

Remarks: Some pathless rough going. Sheep country – keep dogs under control

Public transport: Oban – Ardrishaig and Oban Easdale buses pass along main road at Kilmore Monday – Saturday

EASY ALTERNATIVE

Traffic is generally very light on the road by Loch Nell. The going from the loch to Barran is flat and makes for a very pleasant, picturesque stroll.

3 GLEN FEOCHAN FALLS

The wide curtain waterfall which plunges over 20 feet in Glen Feochan near Kilmore, is one of the area's hidden scenic gems and makes an ideal walking destination in inclement weather. Unnamed and unmarked on any map, it is easily missed. Although it involves 2 miles of road walking to reach the falls, there is little traffic and the glen is a picturesque mix of the pastoral, low craggy hills and forest. You pass the ruins of the late 15th century old Kilmore church. Some windows and arches still survive. There was a large congregation until mass clearances of tenants made way for sheep.

The single track road through the glen is narrow with few passing places and it is impossible to park near the falls. Either park at Loch Nell (as per walk 2) or around the Barran Estate at Kilmore. *(Take care not to obstruct the road at Barran and please do not park on the grass verges which belong to the householders).* Follow the road along the flat floor of Glen Feochan. After 2 miles it crosses the river and begins to climb. A short way up the hill, turn left into a short grassy clearing among a small copse. The sound of the falls will guide you. The river is reached just beyond a gate. This last 150 yards from the road is inclined to be wet and muddy and boots are advised. Return by your outward route.
Easy 4 miles

4 ASCENT OF BEINN GHLAS 1690 ft / 515m

This hill is the highest point of the rough moorland extending east from Kilmore and Glen Feochan and its ascent is ideal for those looking for a peaceful escape for a few hours. This area is little known except to a few anglers searching for quiet hill lochans. There is unlikely to be anyone about, just you, the fauna and flora and the extensive summit panoramas stretching to Mull, the Firth of Lorn and Etive hills.

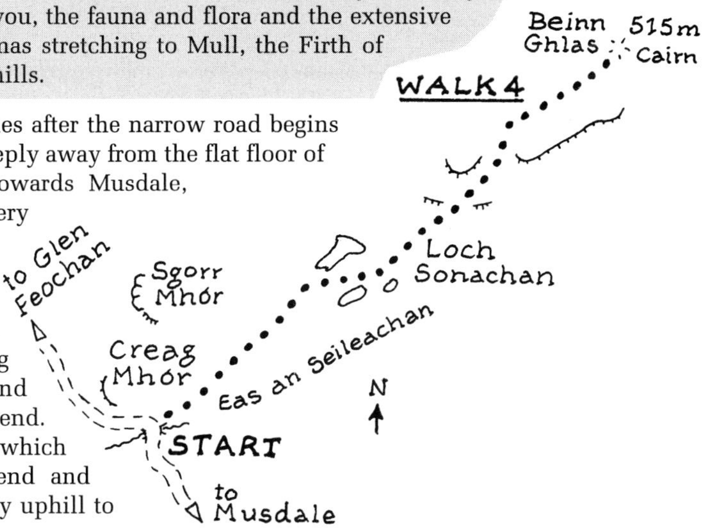

About 1.9 miles after the narrow road begins to climb steeply away from the flat floor of Glen Feochan towards Musdale, the road turns very sharply to the right, crossing a small burn. There is limited roadside parking just before and after the bad bend. Take the path which starts at this bend and heads (NE) gently uphill to

the left of the burn. Within 0.25 mile the path turns to the east. Abandon it and continue north eastward following the floor of the grassy valley until you reach the lochans at the foot of Beinn Ghlas. Keeping the largest lochan on your left, aim for the eastern flanks of the hill. The slopes are initially quite steep but grassy and can be ascended at many points without difficulty. The broad SW ridge is then followed to the summit cairn. There are a number of grassy hummocks and knolls en route which could lead to confusion in mist. In clear conditions the going is straightforward with increasingly enticing views. Return the same way.

FACT FILE

Distance: 5 miles Height gain: 1132 ft / 345m
Time: 3.5 – 4 hours
Start/Finish: GR. 927233 Glen Feochan – Musdale road OS Sheet 49
Remarks: pathless, good navigational skills required in hillfog

5 MINARD POINT

One can easily escape the bustle of Oban and find crowd-free dramatic coastline. Take the A816 Lochgilphead road south out of town and in 2 miles bear left on the narrow road to Kilbride and Lerags. Approximately 3 miles along, there is limited roadside parking just below Lerags Farm. A gentle track begins here, which keeps left of the farm, then bears westward through low rough hills to reach Minard Point in 1.5 miles, at the mouth of Loch Feochan (pronounced 'furkyin'). The environs of Minard House are particularly attractive in early spring when the track is edged with hundreds of daffodils. From the end of the track, narrow paths wend around to the Point, beside huge boulders underneath the cliffs, with views extending to Mull. You may be lucky enough to see otters along the rocky coast. Loch Feochan is a popular haunt and the area around Minard was used in the filming of 'Ring of Bright Water'. To return, retrace your steps, although stronger walkers who don't mind rough going, can venture into the hills above the cliffs for a wider view, before descending towards Lerags Farm.

Easy 3 miles

6 THE ROUND OF KERRERA

This green and hilly island shelters Oban Harbour from the worst of the Atlantic gales. Although lying close to the bustling tourist resort, a walk around Kerrera gives a sense of Hebridean tranquillity and isolation and a taste of early Scottish history. Once used as an old drove road, a winding track loops around the southern two thirds of the island, affording ever changing and enchanting views. Fewer than 50 people now live here, mainly clustered in the north of the island. Away from here, the only sounds you are likely to hear are the breaking surf and cries of the seabirds, curlews and grazing sheep.

Signposts to Gallanach lead from the main square in Oban to the small passenger ferry to Kerrera. From the Kerrera jetty, take the track bearing left along the shore past Horseshoe Bay. Here King Haakon of Norway mustered his great fleet of gal-

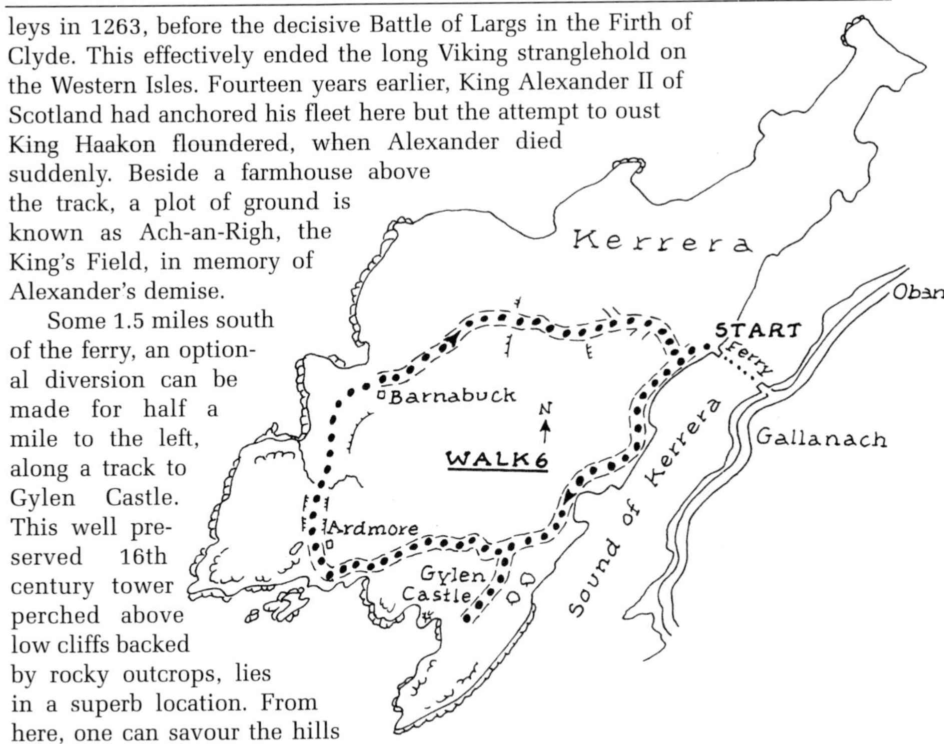

leys in 1263, before the decisive Battle of Largs in the Firth of Clyde. This effectively ended the long Viking stranglehold on the Western Isles. Fourteen years earlier, King Alexander II of Scotland had anchored his fleet here but the attempt to oust King Haakon floundered, when Alexander died suddenly. Beside a farmhouse above the track, a plot of ground is known as Ach-an-Righ, the King's Field, in memory of Alexander's demise.

Some 1.5 miles south of the ferry, an optional diversion can be made for half a mile to the left, along a track to Gylen Castle. This well preserved 16th century tower perched above low cliffs backed by rocky outcrops, lies in a superb location. From here, one can savour the hills of Mull and the lesser islands of the Firth of Lorn. Built as a stronghold for the MacDougalls of Dunollie (whose clan chief still owns much of the island), it was burnt in 1647 by the Covenanting Army under the Marquis of Argyll; the culmination of a series of attacks that had begun the previous year. All the land hereabout was also put to the torch.

Return to the main track and turn left. About 1.25 miles on, a white stone cottage sits in an idyllic setting, looking out to the cliffs and hills of Mull. The path now heads slightly inland between wooden posts, towards a small, narrow, grassy defile, beyond the white cottage at Ardmore (ignore the tracks to the left). At the head of the low pass between small hills, keep to the track on the right side of an overgrown lochan. Keep straight on over a burn at a junction of tracks. At the next junction, keep right and follow the track round the base of a hill. The route now heads inland passing the white farmhouse at Barnabuck. Beyond some ruined cottages, the track begins to climb steadily for approximately 300 feet, giving fine views towards Mull, Lismore and Morvern. As the track begins to descend once more, it passes within 500 yards of the 18th century corn mill at Slaterach. Corn was once a major crop on the island until disastrous crop failures in 1836 and 1837, forced the mill to close.

Keep straight on downhill back to the ferry, passing the tiny school. With pupil numbers reduced to two, it was recently forced to close, a sign of the continuing population decline that began in the 19th century. Returning to the crowds of Oban might be a slight shock to the system after your few hours of idyllic seclusion.

FACT FILE

Distance: 6.5 miles Height gain: 450 ft/137m
Time: 3 - 4 hours
Public Transport: Daily ferry tel: 01631 563665 for further information

7 THE CRUACHAN HORSESHOE

Queening over Loch Awe in stately splendour, Ben Cruachan is a huge but shapely mountain massif comprising a complex of narrow ridges, deeply carved corries and seven tops. The traverse of the five summits encircling the glacial bowl of Cruachan Reservoir provides one of the finest one day hikes in western Scotland and for Munro baggers ticks two off the big list.

There are two alternative routes up to the Cruachan Dam. The shortest and most popular way begins across the road from the Cruachan Power Station on the A82 by Lochawe. *(Limited roadside parking opposite the power station. Parking at the Power Station Visitor Centre is not permitted for non patrons).* A railway bridge spans the Falls of Cruachan Burn. Go under the left hand arch and pick up the poor path climbing very steeply for a thousand feet on the west bank of the burn through a scattering of birch, hazel and oak trees. The path is often boggy especially approaching the dam.

A more gradual alternative is to take the tarmac hydro road from its start near Loch Awe Village. (Parking space just before the locked gate). This adds an extra two miles to the start and finish of the day but is much kinder to those with dodgy knees. Visiting the dam alone makes a pleasant climb for those wanting a minor ascent without venturing onto the mountain itself. The Cruachan Reservoir sits in a dramatic setting with aerial views to the Pass of Brander, Loch Awe and eastward along Glen Lochy to Ben Lui. A mountain bike can be used along the hydro road. In ascent it will probably earn its name of 'push bike' over much of its length but the freewheel downhill after completing the Horseshoe ensures an exhilarating finish to a magnificent day. Just check your brakes first!

From the dam, an east to west traverse is recommended as being navigationally simpler should the mist descend. It also enables one to enjoy for longer, the spectacular views seaward to Loch Linnhe and the Firth of Lorn.

Take the grassy slopes above the eastern shore of the reservoir. Keep low until the stream plunging westwards from the col under Beinn a' Bhuiridh which forms a significant gorge. Beyond, ascend NE slanting across the steep hillside towards the main ridge. Traces of path can ease progress. Once onto the ridge, angles moderate considerably and the going remains predominantly grassy onto the first Munro, Stob Diamh 3272 ft / 998 m. (stob dev), *'peak of the stag.'* On a clear day, the views to the Argyll seaboard and mountains of Lochaber and Lorn, are superb and can extend as far as the Rhum Cuillin, Arran and the Paps of Jura. Ben Cruachan itself forms a grandiose picture, particularly in spring when vestiges of snow cling to the corrie rims, highlighting the sizeable cliffs on the northern flanks.

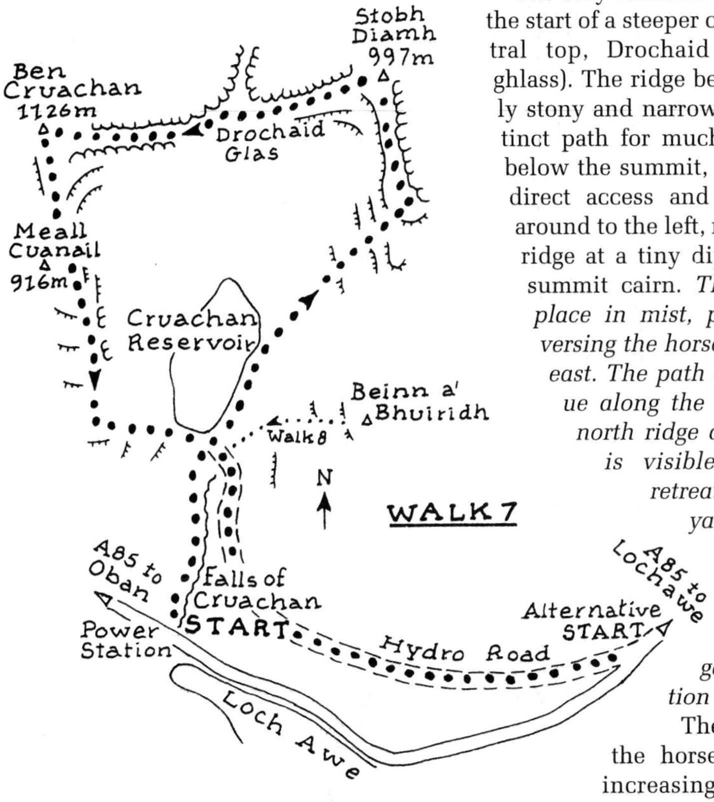

An easy descent leads westward to the start of a steeper climb onto the central top, Drochaid Glas (drochitch ghlass). The ridge becomes increasingly stony and narrow with a fairly distinct path for much of the way. Just below the summit, a line of crags bar direct access and diverts the path around to the left, regaining the main ridge at a tiny dip just west of the summit cairn. *This is a notorious place in mist, particularly if traversing the horseshoe from west to east. The path appears to continue along the steep and narrow north ridge and no other path is visible. One needs to retreat westward for 50 yards from the summit then descend southwards initially before swinging SE, to regain the continuation of the ridge.*

The continuation of the horseshoe eastward is increasingly bouldery, following the narrow ridge crest. Before the final climb onto Ben Cruachan, there is an awkward *mauvais pas,* which can be avoided on the left. Taken direct, the descent to a slight dip in the ridge, over a grooved granite slab, require friction, 'bottom gear' and reasonably long limbs. Some entertaining but straightforward boulder scrambling brings the main summit of Ben Cruachan 3695 ft / 1126 m (byn krooachan) a corruption of Cruachan Beinne, a conical hill atop a broader mountain massif, which describes its shape perfectly. A fine view to the mountains of Mull are added to the previous visual delights.

A steep scrambling descent, on more boulders with traces of path, gains the marshy col under Meall Cuanail (myowl kooaneel). A narrow, muddy path now follows a fence southward. A final short, steep ascent, then it is downhill all the way on a broad grassy ridge. The terrain can be somewhat boggy but the continuing vistas of lochs and islands, offer more than adequate compensation. A series of small crags just above the dam are easily turned and your outward route rejoined.

FACT FILE

Distance: 8 miles (12 miles by hydro road) Height gain: 4500 ft / 1370m

Time: 6 – 8 hours

Start/Finish: on A 82 at GR 079268 or 115266. OS Sheet 50

Remarks: good navigational skills needed in hillfog. Narrow ridges not suitable for the inexperienced under winter conditions.
Public Transport: Oban – Dalmally buses pass both starts. Trains stop at Lochawe. Usually there are no access problems in stalking season by these routes.
EASIER ALTERNATIVE
If walking only to Cruachan dam via hydro road, 6 miles on tarmac road and 1000 feet of ascent is entailed.
See also end of walk 8

8 THE TRAVERSE OF BEINN A' BHUIRIDH 896 m / 2941 ft

This shapely Corbett is rather neglected, being the southward extension of the Cruachan Horseshoe which only the very hardiest of walkers include in the full circuit. However, it is a fine hill in its own right, worthy of a separate expedition. Try and save for a fine day since as a viewpoint it can rival anything the adjacent horseshoe can offer and in mist may present route finding difficulties, particularly in descent. Being a mere 18 metres short of the 'magical' Munro height, it possesses the added attraction of being devoid of crowds. I have climbed it in August and not met another soul. During the autumn the peak may well live up to its name, (byn a vooree) the *'hill of the roaring',* when the mountains and glens resound to the bellowing of rutting stags.

There is limited parking on the Glen Strae B8077 road at its junction with the A85. A track which once served a mineral quarry now leads round to the north side of Monadh Driseig, the eastern flank of Beinn a' Bhuiridh where moderate grassy slopes provide straightforward access to the ridge above. The going is somewhat marshy underfoot, enlivened by a colourful matting of orchids, bog asphodel and butterwort. *(Alternatively the grassy southern slopes of Monadh Driseig can be tackled but the gradients are more severe and not recommended).*

The broad ridge leads gently up over a series of hummocks and knolls with boggy depressions between. This necessitates a far from straight, drunken course and could lead to confusion in mist. The northern flanks fall dramatically to the Allt Coire Ghlais in a series of sizeable cliffs and clefts. Northward, the view is filled by the complexities of Ben Cruachan and its neighbouring Munros. Elsewhere the panorama is far reaching, extending to the Border hills way beyond the Arrochar Alps, down Loch Awe to the Isles of Arran and Jura and along the watery length of the Strath of Orchy and Glen Lochy to Ben Lui.

Steeper slopes gain the first cairn. The Island of Mull and the glorious Lorn coast now hove into view along the final short hummocky ridge leading to the second cairn and true summit.

If you can draw yourself away, there are three options in descent. The shortest route of descent would be to retrace one's steps and in mist is probably the safest. In clear conditions however, a less direct but easier circular route is possible with a descent via the Cruachan Reservoir and hydro road. Descend towards the hydro road down steep grassy slopes, initially in a westerly direction. Stray too far right, a line of broken crags await. Once off the really steep section, swing round towards

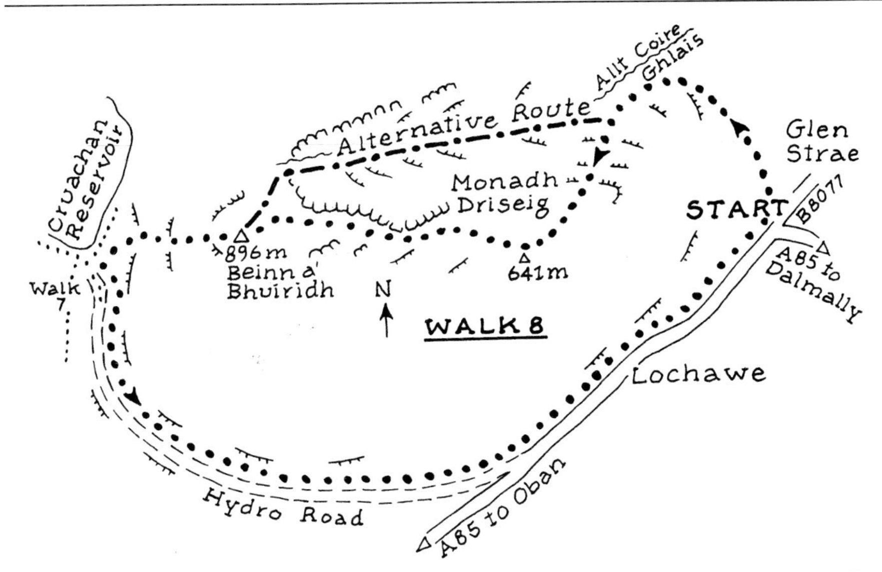

the dam over more gradual ground. The final drop to the road just below the dam is again steep but well stepped grass makes for safe if slow progress. Do not attempt to descend directly to the hydro road away from the dam since cliffs and very precipitous slopes rim much of the road. The aerial view of Loch Awe, Strath of Orchy, Glen Lochy and the Pass of Brander will be savoured as you follow the tarmaced road back down to the A85, 1.5 miles from your starting point.

Alternatively, if you don't fancy road walking, although not obvious from above, there is a fairly direct route descending very steeply northward for some thousand feet from the summit to the Larig Torran col. Cattle herders used to drive their beasts eastwards over this pass to graze on the floor of the huge corrie now swallowed up by the Cruachan Reservoir. From the col, descend into wild Coire Glas underneath the northern cliffs of Beinn a' Bhuiridh and follow the south bank of the Allt Coire Ghlais back towards your start point.

FACT FILE

Distance: 10 miles Height gain: 3000 feet / 914m
Time: 5 – 7 hours
Remarks: virtually pathless, good navigational skills essential.
Start / Finish: Junction A85/B8077 GR 133283 OS Sheet 50
Public Transport: Buses ply along the A85 between Oban and Dalmally
Stalking season: Notices put up daily by Castles Estate who request the hill is avoided 20 Sept – 20 Oct. Dogs not welcome

EASY ALTERNATIVE – GLEN STRAE FALLS

Drive along the B8077 towards the road bridge over the River Strae. There are parking spaces just before the bridge. A Land - Rover track with just a little gentle climbing follows the course of the River Strae. Wild Glen Strae is a typical U shaped glacial valley with a stepped valley floor and wide river surrounded by high hills with broken crags and numerous sidestreams, best seen just after heavy rain. A thousand yards up the glen, you can opt to leave the main track and cross the river at the bridge, then follow the path on the east bank of the river for a mile to the very attractive waterfalls marked on the map at GR 165313. Here the Strae is joined by its main tributary cascading down from Ben Donachain. There are a series of falls on both rivers and a small gorge. The path and Land Rover track continue up the valley for about another mile beyond the falls should you wish a longer leg stretch. This gentle walk is perfectly safe to do in the rain and providing you are properly clad, can be enjoyed however inclement the weather, given all the fluvial activity in the vicinity.

Distance optional, 3.5 miles for waterfalls walk

SHORT ASCENTS IN THE DALMALLY AREA

8A MONUMENT HILL FROM DALMALLY

Just to the west of Dalmally railway station, a public road climbs to a pass just below Monument Hill. It is more rewarding however to make the 300 foot climb on foot, to really appreciate the beautiful banks of flowers to either side of the road and the splendid views to the surrounding mountains, and the northern end of Loch Awe with Kilchurn Castle directly below. The hilltop was the site of an ancient fort but today is dominated by the huge monument to Duncan Ban MacIntryre, the celebrated 18th century Gaelic poet. Beside the memorial is a curious flat stone engraved with a cross, whose origins are a mystery.

Distance 2.75 miles

8B ASCENT OF CREAG MHOR

Another short hillwalk in the vicinity offers equally fine views but without the disturbance of motorists. Creag Mhor near the foot of Glen Strae, is a good example of a volcanic dyke. Amongst the heather on its western shoulder, lie the ruins of Tigh Mor, once a MacGregor stronghold until they were ousted from the glen in the 14th century, having made themselves unpopular with Edward I.

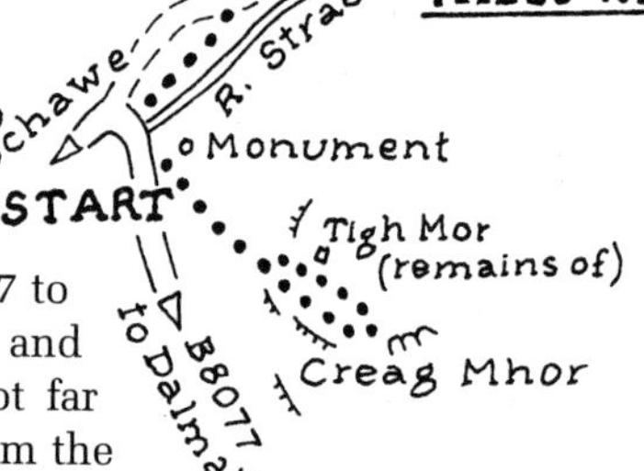

From Dalmally or Lochawe, take the B8077 to the 2 river bridges which lie close together and mark the entrance to Glen Strae (parking not far along on the Lochawe side of the bridge). From the bridges, walk up the road towards Stronmilchan for about 150 yards. Turn left up a private track through a kissing gate and climb to an impressive stone monument dedicated to Duncan McLaren, a Victorian MP and Lord Provost of Edinburgh. It stands in a panoramic setting above scattered Scots pine, dwarfed by the mighty bulk of Ben Cruachan's eastern tops and Beinn Eunaich with its dramatic waterfall cutting a long white swathe above Castles Farm.

Retrace your steps some 70 yards then bear left along a vague track heading roughly in the direction of crag topped Creag Mhor. Go through a gateway and continue straight ahead, keeping the fence to your right. The going can be somewhat marshy here. Where the fence takes a definite turn to the left, follow it a short way to a stile beyond a low barbed wire fence. The latter is easily ducked under at present but a newspaper may be handy in case it needs to be straddled over in future. Beyond, pathless, rough but drier slopes of heather moorland, lead without difficulty onto Creag Mhor. The electricity pylons which intruded earlier, are much less invasive here and the views of Strath Orchy and over Kilchurn Castle to Loch Awe, are enchanting.

Having explored the remains of Tigh Mor which lie just to the north, aim back down to the stile and your outward route.

FACT FILE

Distance: 2 miles, Height gain: 600 ft/ 183m, Time: 1.5 hours

Remarks: The route passes through grazing sheep. Dogs unwelcome on Castles Estate.

9 ASCENT OF BEINN LORA 1010 ft / 308m

Named after an early Celtic hero, Laoighre, this hill dominates the small village of Benderloch some 9 miles north of Oban. Although the short ascent itself lacks excitement, being largely a trudge through coniferous forest, the summit views are superb from such a low hill.

A waymarked path begins at a small, signed car park near the south end of Benderloch. The path soon divides, joining up again in about a mile. The path to the right gives the easier ascent through the dense forest, though is still often quite steep. Just beyond a limited viewpoint, turn right at the junction of paths. A short gentle section is followed by a short steep slope, near the top of which, a signed diversion leads in 100 yards to another viewpoint. The going now eases dramatically until the forest edge is reached. Beyond the fence and gate is a picnic table and a fine view westward to the Firth of Lorn. The good track ends here. An increasingly boggy path now heads eastward over open moorland to the summit. A short flat area before the final climb is usually very wet. Slightly higher ground on the right, offers a drier route. From the summit, there are extensive panoramic vistas to Mull across the

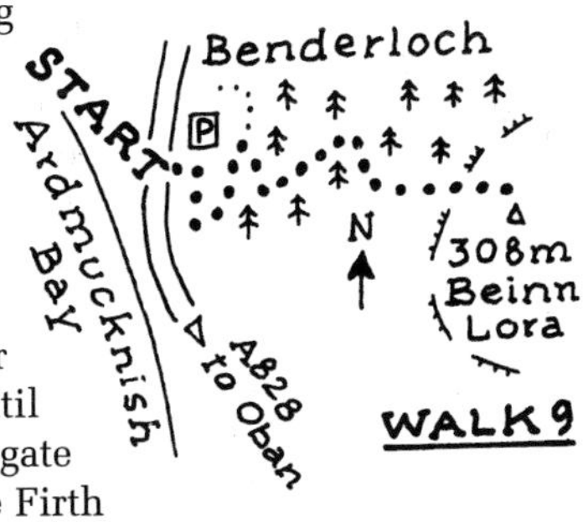

Firth of Lorn and to Loch Linnhe, Ben Cruachan and the Loch Creran hills. Return by the same route.
Distance: 4 miles Height gain: 1100 feet Time: 2 – 3 hours
Public transport: numerous buses from Oban and Fort William serve Benderloch.

10 SUTHERLAND'S GROVE

Just north of Barcaldine on the A828 near Loch Creran, the Forestry Commission has laid out four easy to follow waymarked walking trails and two longer cycling or wayfarers' trails, ideal when the weather is too inclement for the hills. Unlike most forestry plantations, there is generally an absence of monotonous coniferous stands. Instead there is delightful mixed broad-leaved woodland with oak, birch, beech, rowan and Victorian Douglas Firs combined with the more traditional forestry trees of larch and spruce.

The four walking trails vary in length from 0.75 mile to 2 miles. All initially climb a rather rough path above a dramatic small wooded gorge, through which the Abhainn Teithil plunges in spectacular fashion, particularly after heavy rain. Above the gorge, the trails diverge and follow tracks which are much easier underfoot. The hardest walk is the green marked 'fishermens' trail'; climbing for some 400 feet to the Glen Dubh Reservoir, from which there are attractive views of the hills of the Lynn of Lorne National Scenic Area.

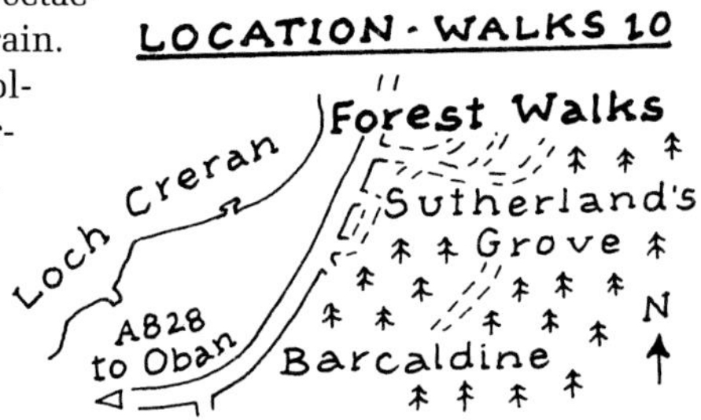

The 5 mile and 7 mile cycling/wayfaring trails keep to the broad forestry roads, missing the fine gorge. They occasionally afford some good vistas of the surrounding hills and loch though these may change in future, being dependant on the growth of the trees and the extent of felling.
Public transport: numerous buses from Oban and Fort William serve Barcaldine.

11 THE ASCENT OF CREACH BHEINN 810m / 2656 ft

Although standing in the shadow of the adjacent Munro Beinn Sgurlaird, this fine Corbett is a stunning vantage point for the western hills and seaboard and offers a quiet ascent with birds of prey likely to be your only companions. Also, much less height gain is entailed compared to the Munro and the botanical interest is more varied.

Creach Bheinn (pro: krech vyn) translates as the hill of spoil or plunder. For many centuries, reiving cattle from neighbouring clans was something of a national pastime in Scotland. However, apart from its lower flanks to the east, the generally steep flanks of the mountain do not seem conducive to the grazing and hiding of stolen cattle. Possibly the name stems from one particular raid but like so many Scottish hill names, the origins are shrouded in mystery.

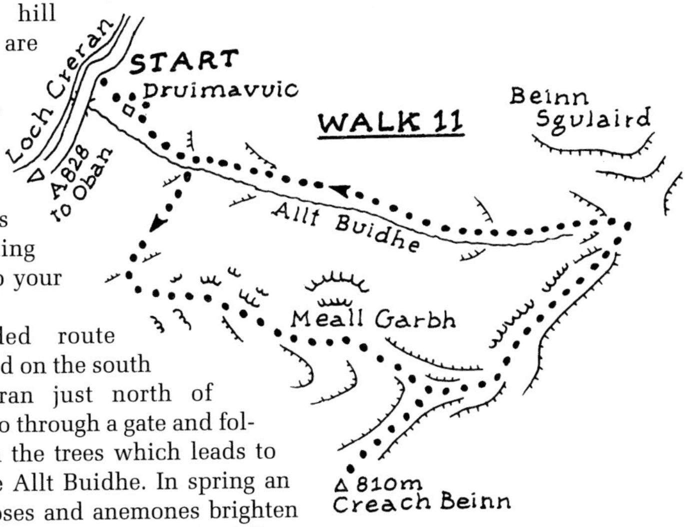

More recently, mass afforestation on the lower flanks has reduced the walking route options considerably, assuming that you want to keep your sanity!

The recommended route starts on the A828 road on the south shore of Loch Creran just north of Druimavuic House. Go through a gate and follow the path through the trees which leads to the north bank of the Allt Buidhe. In spring an exuberance of primroses and anemones brighten your way. Whilst higher up the mountain, following the course of the streams and protruding from under the many broken crags, an abundance of alpine flora runs rampant into the height of summer. Saxifrage is especially common, including the low mat forming purple saxifrage which is often actually pale pink in colour and the longer stemmed starry saxifrage.

Once clear of the trees, continue for a short distance along the river then cross over and work your way to the west over open grass and heather moorland to connect with the initially steep WNW ridge of Meall Garbh. Although this translates as rough hill, the actual crest of the ridge comprises straightforward moorland, scattered boulders and the occasional small rock outcrop. Most of the granite crags are quite broken and flank the northern slopes above the Allt Buidhe. Above 500m/1640 ft the vegetation shortens and the gradient eases considerably and apart from one short steeper section, remains moderate up to the NE Top. An exceedingly gentle ridge then leads in a thousand yards to the main summit cairn.

The intimate seaward views to the west are extensive throughout much of the ascent and culminate in a superb summit panorama to the islands of Mull, Eriska and Lismore beyond Loch Creran, the hills of Morvern and Ardgour fronted by Loch Linnhe and to beautiful Loch Etive.

To descend, return to the NE Top then drop steeply east before swinging NE more gently on a well defined ridge above broken crags. From the wide col under Beinn Sgulaird, turn down the north bank of the Allt Buidhe back to the start point. An intermittent and barely discernible path, becomes clearer with loss of height.

FACT FILE

Distance: 7.5 miles Height gain: 2658ft / 810m

Time: 4 – 5 hours

Remarks: some pathless sections, good navigational skills required in hillfog

Start / Finish: GR 007451 OS 1:50,000 Sheet 50

Public Transport: Oban to Fort William buses pass along Loch Creran

Stalking Season Contact Ardchattan estate Tel. 01631 710274. Estate requests the hill be avoided 15 Sept – 15 Oct.

EASY ALTERNATIVE

Where the A828 road bends very sharply to the left about half a mile north of Druimavuic House (GR 011456) a very gentle track starts, following the course of the river along Glen Ure towards Glenure House. The track eventually narrows to a path but the going remains very easy if sometimes stony or muddy. The combination of scattered woodland, the wide river, the surrounding knobbly and occasionally craggy mountains and after a mile, the small Loch Baile Mhic Chailein, make for a very pleasant walk at any time of year. I have even enjoyed it on a freezing cold Boxing Day with the bare trees and lack of flowers. In spring it is particularly delightful with the flora burgeoning into life and the glen resounding to the cuckoo, buzzards and sparrow-hawks. I have even seen an otter several miles upstream when the river was in a state of flood. If you walk as far as Glenure House, it is possible to make a circular return by the track to Elleric and along the very quiet road on the north side of the glen. However, the road is shut in by trees for most of its length, so I recommend retracing your steps back along the path. *Distance optional, maximum mileage 6 miles.*

12 BEN STARAV 3541ft/1078m, BEINN NAN AIGHENAN 3141 ft/957m, GLAS BHEINN MHOR 3258 ft/997m

The walk describes the ascent of three of the fine Etive Munros. Only the most energetic and ardent of Munro baggers are likely to complete the traverse in one expedition. The average walker will prefer to split it up into two or even three walks. For those who have managed to avoid the contagious Munro disease and just want to enjoy an excellent hillwalk with entrancing far reaching views, dramatic river scenery and an interesting route over a striking mountain, then Ben Starav alone is a must. All options are considered.

All recommended routes begin in Glen Etive some two miles NE of the road end where there is limited parking. Take the track to Coileitir Cottage leading down to the River Etive and cross the bridge. On a fine summer day, this provides an enchanting start. Purple scabious carpet the bordering grass, patrolled by clacking wheatears and flitting meadow brown butterflies. Sandpipers glide over the almost still waters reflecting the mountains above and the birches lining the banks.

Beyond the cottage, a boggy path leads quickly to the Allt Mheuran. Cross over the bridge a little way upstream. Follow a rather wet path on the west bank for some 500 yards, then head up the broad, increasingly drier slopes of the 2 mile long, steep, north ridge of Ben Starav. A narrow path on the crest of the ridge, carves through the grass, heather and a colourful array of flowers. An impressive view opens up northward along Glen Etive. The ridge becomes increasingly stony and narrower, with precipitous slopes falling away on either side. The final few hundred feet comprise steep rocky slopes littered with granite boulders which allow for some entertaining wee scrambles and boulder hopping.

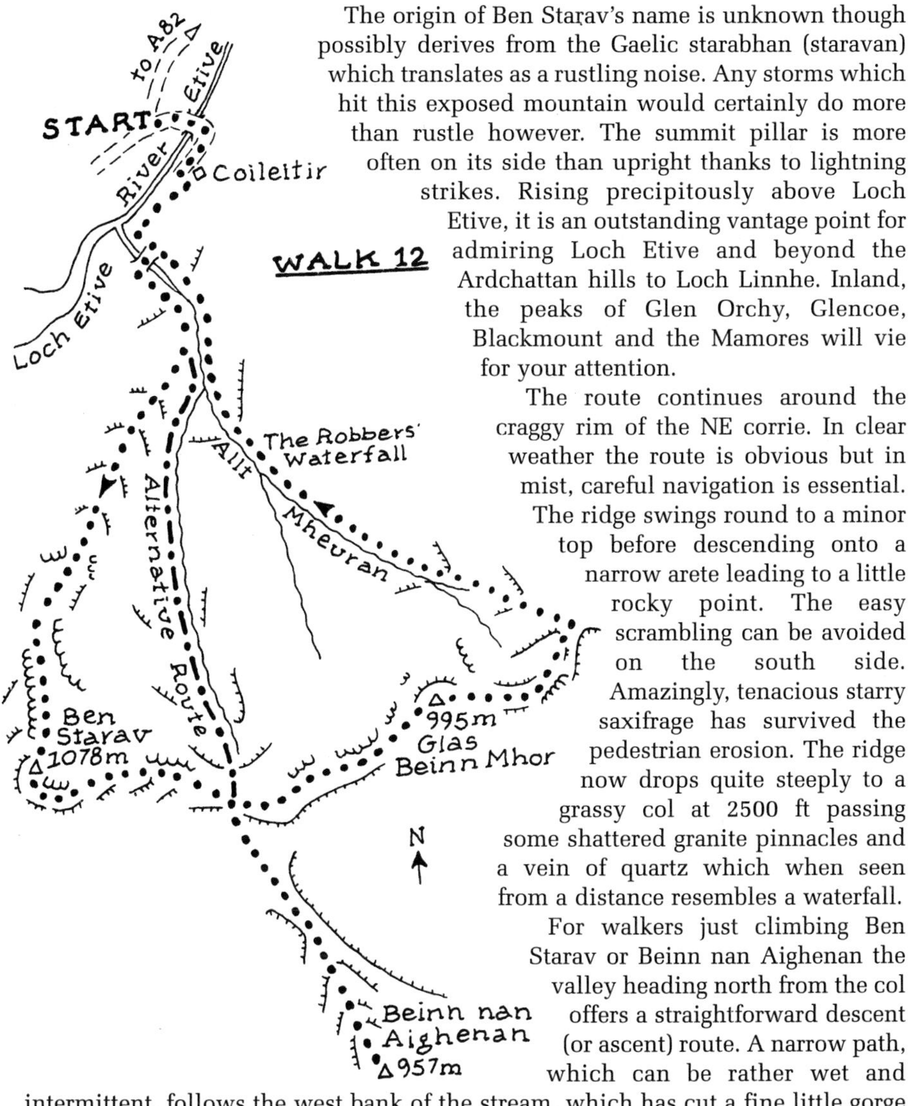

The origin of Ben Starav's name is unknown though possibly derives from the Gaelic starabhan (staravan) which translates as a rustling noise. Any storms which hit this exposed mountain would certainly do more than rustle however. The summit pillar is more often on its side than upright thanks to lightning strikes. Rising precipitously above Loch Etive, it is an outstanding vantage point for admiring Loch Etive and beyond the Ardchattan hills to Loch Linnhe. Inland, the peaks of Glen Orchy, Glencoe, Blackmount and the Mamores will vie for your attention.

The route continues around the craggy rim of the NE corrie. In clear weather the route is obvious but in mist, careful navigation is essential. The ridge swings round to a minor top before descending onto a narrow arete leading to a little rocky point. The easy scrambling can be avoided on the south side. Amazingly, tenacious starry saxifrage has survived the pedestrian erosion. The ridge now drops quite steeply to a grassy col at 2500 ft passing some shattered granite pinnacles and a vein of quartz which when seen from a distance resembles a waterfall.

For walkers just climbing Ben Starav or Beinn nan Aighenan the valley heading north from the col offers a straightforward descent (or ascent) route. A narrow path, which can be rather wet and intermittent, follows the west bank of the stream, which has cut a fine little gorge with an attractive series of falls, just above its confluence with the Allt Mheuran. At the confluence, the main stream plunges 50 ft in a fine double waterfall, into a precipitous gorge (the Robbers' Waterfall, misnamed on some maps as being further upstream). The path then leads back above the river to Coileitir.

From the col, keen Munroists may wish to detour to Beinn nan Aighenan, (byn an yanan) *'hill of the hinds'*, a peak rather sent to Coventry by the other Etive hills. Solitude is almost guaranteed once you begin a 500 ft descent of pathless, rough, grassy slopes, leading to a cluster of tiny lochans and another col. An easy, though steep ascent for 1150 ft up the NNW ridge, brings the summit. A clear path emerges out of the grass some 200 ft into the climb and wends a way between a series of tiny crags. The summit is a good viewpoint for the whole of the long and lonely Glen Kinglass with the Orchy hills beyond.

Having returned to the col under Glas Bheinn Mhor, (glas ven voar) a grassy plod leads over a minor top. A broad, rockier ridge then leads towards the summit of the third Munro, the *'big grey-green hill'*. The excellent panoramas continue as you descend the narrower east ridge. Gentle at first, there is a short, steep clambering drop to the col at the head of Glen Mheuran, which is easier slightly to the right. It is now simply a matter of following the beautiful Allt Mheuran down to Coileitir. Initially pathless and marshy, a narrow path soon develops above the north bank. A succession of spectacular small falls and waterslides are gloriously set out below the craggy southern flanks of Glas Bheinn Mhor, whilst ahead of you lie the Glencoe peaks. A slight detour to see the aforementioned Robbers' Waterfall is worthwhile. A fitting finale to a grand walk.

FACT FILE

Distance: ***Ben Starav*** *only: 7.5 miles Height gain 3610 ft / 1100m (5 – 6hrs)*
Ben Starav & Glas Bheinn Mhor: *10 miles, 4550ft / 1386m (7 – 8hrs)*
All 3 Munros: *13 miles 6200ft / 1889m (8 – 10 hrs)*
Start/Finish: Glen Etive near Coileitir GR 137467 OS Sheet 50
Remarks: given the narrowness of some ridges, Ben Starav is not recommended in high winds, or for the inexperienced, under winter conditions
Public Transport: postbus once a day runs from Fort William to Glen Etive
Stalking season: contact Glen Etive estate 01855 851277 who request the hills are avoided Sept – mid Oct, and that dogs are kept on leads at all times.

13 THE ASCENT OF BEINN TRILLEACHAN 839m / 2754 ft

Driving down Glen Etive, the view is increasingly filled by the dramatic and distinctive shaped Corbett, Beinn Trilleachan (byn tree lyochan), whose 700 foot granite 'Etive' slabs plunge spectacularly towards Loch Etive. In sunshine, this climbers' playground sparkles like silver. *'The mountain of sandpipers or oyster catchers'* is named after the trilling birds who haunt the sheltered sea loch and are often seen close to shore, their gliding wings barely skimming the calm waters. Botanists too will find plenty to interest them en route.

The ascent begins at the forest edge just beyond the house at Gualachulain, about 400 yards before the road ends. Following close to the forest fence take a little used path NW (unmarked on map) leading over to Glen Ure. It is often quite boggy underfoot and gaiters are useful. After some 650 feet of ascent, the path levels out. One can leave the path here and tackle the steep grassy slopes onto the north east ridge of the mountain. However, the vegetation is not so deep and steep if one follows the flat section of the path for a further 400 yards before cutting up onto the ridge. There are less small crags to weave around too although the going is still rough underfoot and one has to beware of the numerous foot catching small pot holes hidden in the grass. In late spring and summer botanists will not want to hurry. Amongst the various grasses and common eyebright, thyme, bog asphodel and tormentil, lurk a number of orchids including the early purple, early marsh and common spotted and the comparatively rare butterfly orchids. The growing view to the Glencoe peaks and the environs of Loch Etive also provide a feast for the eyes.

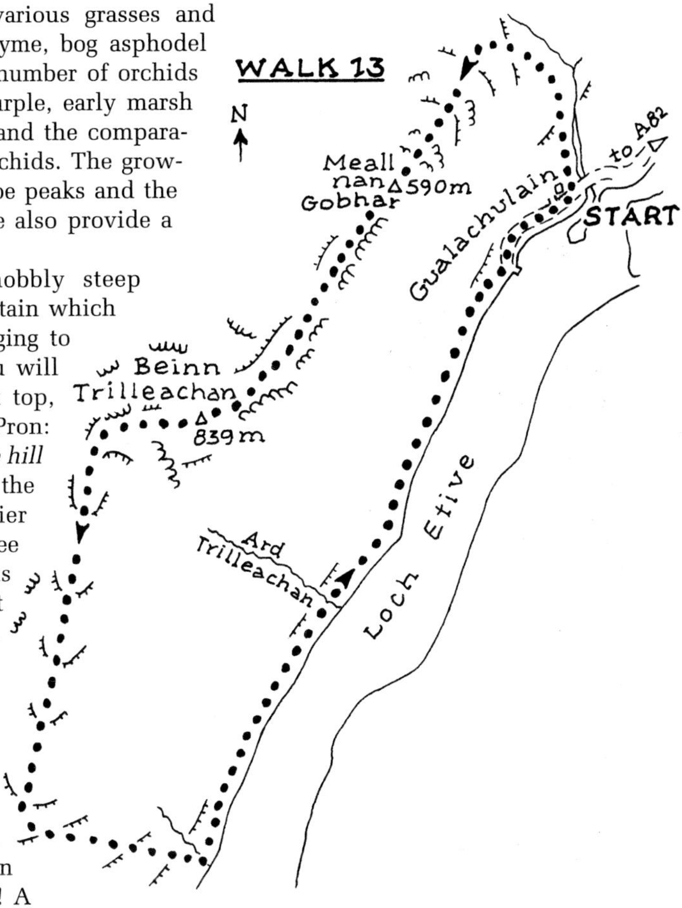

Following the knobbly steep backbone of the mountain which likens to limpets clinging to an upturned boat, you will barely notice the first top, Meall non Gobhar (Pron: myowl nan gowar) *'the hill of the goats'*. Beyond, the ridge becomes rockier with the occasional wee granite tor. Gradients eventually relent at around 2300 feet. Increasingly, you will become aware of the exposure from the great eastern slabs out of sight below, above which the next top is airily perched. This is no place to be in a strong westerly gale! A steep descent for some 250 feet beyond this top, leads to a gentler mile long ridge which is less exposed. From the summit, the views of Loch Etive are dramatic. In winter and spring, given the afforestation smothering the lower flanks of the mountains and the shapeliness of the snow capped peaks, it is a scene rather reminiscent of the Canadian Rockies on a miniature scale. Behind you, the view to the peaks of Glenure and the Blackmount are equally impressive.

The quickest way to descend is to retrace your steps. A more interesting though longer way is to make a linear traverse. Descend the crest of the moderately graded southern ridge until well beyond the Ard Trilleachan stream. Given the crags which flank the eastern slopes for some distance, non scramblers are advised to keep to the ridge until just before it suddenly steepens around the 400 metre mark, then turn down to Loch Etive, threading a way through the scattered woodland.

A path leads back to the start point just above the shore of the loch. The going underfoot can be rather wet and is very variable from good turf to rougher bog and a boulder hop, so progress is unlikely to be rapid. In compensation are the frequent attractive settings through which you pass. To the accompaniment of the insistent 'kleep' of sandpipers, the surrounding hills and loch are often framed through a delightful scattering of oak, holly, alder, birch, Scots pine and dwarf willow trees with a variety of ferns, mosses, liverworts and other bog loving plants at your feet. This section of the shore has been designated a Site of Special Scientific Interest. The path also passes under the dramatic pink/grey 'Etive' slabs, down which plunge numerous often spectacular burns, concluding an excellent and varied walk.

FACT FILE

Distance: 8.5 miles Height gain: 3070 ft / 935m
Time: 5.5 – 7 hours
Start / Finish: GR 112454 OS Sheet 50
Remarks: not advised in high winds or under snow conditions except for the highly experienced
Public Transport: post bus runs along Glen Etive once a day.
Stalking Season: Contact Forest Enterprise Tel. 01631 566155.

EASIER WALKS AROUND LOCH ETIVE

13A This magnificent loch stretches for 18 miles but for much of its length has no road alongside. The only way to explore is by foot or boat. One of the finest stretches is that mentioned above at the end of the Beinn Trilleachan walk. The gradient is gentle but as already intimated is inclined to be wet and rough in places. The first three miles from the roadhead is recommended, returning the same way.

13B The path following the north eastern side of the loch is generally less rough, though after a fine beginning, lacks the arboreal and fauna interest of the north west shore. The Etive slabs however are well viewed across the loch, especially when caught by the morning sun. It also allows for an optional diversion to the impressively situated Robbers Waterfall on the Allt Mheuran. Take the track down to Coileitir Cottage, some 2 miles NE of the road end in Glen Etive and follow the path to the Allt Mheuran (as per Ben Starav walk). The path up to the waterfall which cuts across the lower flanks of Ben Starav's north ridge, entails some 400 feet of easy climbing. Having retraced your steps to the bridge over the Allt Mheuran, a path follows the stream down to the River Etive and in a mile reaches the loch shore. The path continues for another 11 miles to Inverawe, although most walkers will settle for a mile or two before retracing their steps, walking under the precipitous western flanks of Ben Starav, deeply riven by foaming burns.

13C The southern end of the loch offers equally fine walking on both sides. Some 2 miles east of Taynuilt on the A85 Oban to Tyndrum road, a road crosses the River Awe and leads to Inverawe (park at Inverawe Country Park). The public road soon ends but a good undulating farm road leads along the south east shore under the shapely Taynuilt Peak of Ben Cruachan. There are often steep drops to the loch from the track and grand views of the surrounding hills and side valleys. If you have the energy to walk the 5 miles to Ardmaddy, you will come across the remains of an iron furnace built in 1723. Fortunately strict rules were laid down over the timber felling to feed this furnace and the Bonawe Furnace near Taynuilt, hence the many beautiful tracts of natural woodland still surviving along the loch.

13D The last alternative is to to take the minor road off the A828 at North Connel and follow the north shore of Loch Etive to almost the road end at Bonawe. There is plenty of parking 200 yards before the Bonawe Quarry. An excellent undulating track follows the lochshore eastward. The first half a mile goes through the quarry itself. There is usually no restriction on pedestrian access unless they are blasting. It is preferable to walk through on a long summer evening or at the weekend when work is finished. It can be quite interesting to see work in progress but the dust clouds from all the lorries can be unpleasant. Once clear of the quarry, the scenery is delightful as the track wends through woodland with frequent beautiful views of the loch and surrounding mountains. The 3 miles to Cadderlie are recommended. *Note: buses run from Oban to Bonawe Mon – Sat.*

For those with the energy for a short hillwalk, the ascent of **Beinn Duirinnnis** 1821 ft / 555m affords stunning and extensive panoramas including virtually the whole of Loch Etive and westward to the high hills of Mull. Just before the single house at Craig, some 1.5 miles along the shore from Bonawe, a small burn flows down under the track. From here, traces of a path climbs up through scattered woodland soon reaching open ground. The bracken gives way to essentially grassy slopes with occasional small crags to weave through. In clear weather, route selection is straightforward. The steepening west ridge is followed to the summit. It is easiest to return the same way as its other flanks are exceedingly steep.
Distance: 5 miles Height gain: 1800 ft / 550 m Time: 4 hours

14 WALKS FROM CUIL

Beautiful Cuil Bay lies just off the A828 some 6 miles north of Appin; a scenic gem that most tourists miss as they rush along the main road. Several short fine walks begin at the turning circle a mile along the narrow single track road, beyond the scattered white painted houses of South Cuil (ample parking along the roadside). On a clear day, there are stunning views along Loch Linnhe to innumerable small islands and westwards to the rough mountains of Ardgour. Inland, the slopes of Beinn a' Bheithir and Fraochaidh, rise in stately splendour.

Don't be tempted by the path shown on the OS map which starts near Greenfield Farm and swings north eastward towards Ardsheal House. The views from the path are excellent but the going underfoot is usually atrociously wet and boggy. There are better alternatives.

For those desiring a flat walk, take the track from the turning circle following the shoreline north westward. At the first path junction, bear left to reach an old stone cottage. From here one can follow the shoreline on a vague track. After 100 yards however, it necessitates a small clamber through a broken rocky outcrop above the sea which can be very slippery when wet. An easier way from the cot-

tage takes the track to the right up a short rise, then turns left onto a grassy track which runs parallel to the shore. From this point is flat but can be a bit rough and marshy after rain and at such times is usually easier beside the shore once past the rock outcrop. Continue straight ahead and beyond a burn, ascend the very low knolls of glacial moraine for the uninterrupted view across Loch Linnhe to striking Garbh Bheinn and other equally fine mountains of Ardgour. Return by the same route.
2 miles maximum.

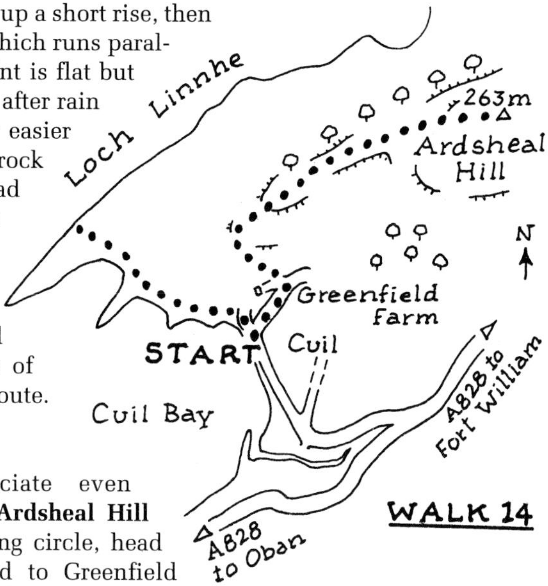

HILLWALKERS can appreciate even grander vistas by ascending **Ardsheal Hill** 864ft / 263m. From the turning circle, head inland along the tarmac road to Greenfield Farm. At the junction of 4 tracks at the road end, turn left then immediately right. Go through the gate and turn left uphill for 100 yards. Just round the crown of a right bend, fork left and cross the burn. Continue straight ahead on a grassy track, avoiding the more obvious track on the left. Climb gently uphill for 200 yards to a gate, then through a gap in a dilapidated wall just ahead. Turn right and climb the rough moorland slopes onto the mile long, straightforward SW ridge of Ardsheal Hill which is followed to the summit. Your moorland trudge will be rewarded with electrifying views along much of Loch Linnhe. Return by your outward route.
3.5 miles: Height gain: 864 ft / 263m: 2 hours
Public transport: Oban – Fort William buses pass through Duror, 1 mile from Cuil.

15 THE BEINN A' BHEITHIR HORSESHOE

Beinn a' Bheithir (pron: byn a vair) *'the hill of the thunderbolt'*, dominates the mouth of Loch Leven where it flows into Loch Linnhe. The horseshoe encompasses two fine Munros and a smaller top, enclosing wild, north facing corries, well displayed when approaching Ballachulish from the north. Justifiably, the traverse is growing in popularity, having a reputation for being a magnificent vantage point for Lochaber and the west coast.

Heavy afforestation of the lower half of the mountain dictates the possible routes to the stonier summits. If transport can be arranged, an east-west traverse from Ballachulish to Kentallon pier is preferable because of the interest of route and ever changing and finer panoramas. The alternative horseshoe traverse from Ballachulish descending via Gleann a' Chaolais also provides a fine circuit.

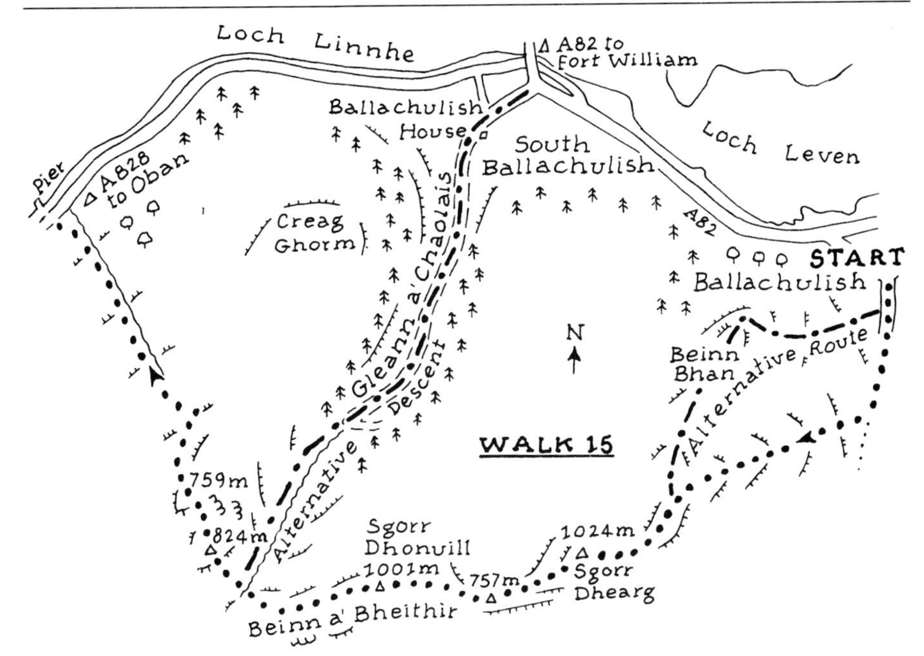

Both options are described.

Do not be tempted by suggestions of reaching the north ridge of Sgorr Bhan or Sgorr Bheag from the Allt Guibhaschain. I met a walker who woefully recounted the nightmare of fighting a way through endless forest, forcing him to crawl on all fours at one point through the tangle of trees!

From Ballachulish village, follow the signed 'footpath to Glen Creran'. Non scramblers should head westwards up pathless grass and heather slopes onto the north ridge of Sgorr Bhan. On reaching the crest, gradients ease dramatically and a path appears. The increasingly stony ridge is then followed easily to the summit.

Providing one has a good head for heights, an infinitely more interesting approach keeps on the Glen Creran path to the foot of the NE ridge of Sgorr Ban. This narrows to a rocky arete requiring some easy but exhilarating scrambling to surmount. From Sgorr Bhan the glaciated Pass of Glencoe appears as an interesting series of U shapes set one inside another. The eagles-eye glimpse of the Ballachulish Bridge way below with Loch Linnhe beyond and the striking view of the Mamores fronted by Loch Leven, will also help dispel any thoughts of tiredness.

Beyond the summit, the first Munro of the day is easily gained along a delightful narrow, curving ridge rimming one of the large northern glacial bowls. It is surprising to find sheep grazing so high, there being little vegetation in evidence. Ptarmigan and buzzards too seem to thrive, inspite of the apparent desolation. The name Sgorr Dhearg, *'red peak'* (skor jerrrak) 3361 ft / 1024 m, is a reflection of the pink quartzite rocks which dominate its upper reaches.

Eroded stony slopes give way to easier grass and a col at 757 metres. Beyond, the path climbs steeply. Hugging the edge of the northern granite cliffs, it provides an airy finish to the ascent of the second Munro. The sweeping coastal vistas of Loch Linnhe and the rugged mountains of Ardgour and Morvern are ones to savour from the summit of Sgorr Dhonuill 3285 ft / 1001m (skor ghawil). *'Donald's Peak'* is named in memory of the surviving Macdonalds fleeing from the infamous massacre of Glencoe. Scantily clad and at night in a blizzard, they crossed these mountains to the safety of Glen Duror. A humbling thought to those of us who brave the hills today decked out in all the latest high-tech finery.

There are three feasible lines of descent. Least interesting but the quickest if bad weather dictates a hasty retreat, involves a return to the col between the two Munros. Descend the steep rough ground to the north west on the west side of a small stream flowing into the forest. A track can be picked up in Gleann a' Chaolais on the west bank of the main river leading to Ballachulish House. The A82 is then followed for 1.5. miles back to Ballachulish.

A more interesting route into Gleann a' Chaolais, descends gentle stony slopes westward from Sgorr Dhonuill for a mile until there is a break in the steep craggy ground to the north. Below a dip in the ridge, the far side of a small flat-topped knoll, a grassy gully leads down towards the forest and the aforementioned track along the stream to Ballachulish House.

For those completing the full traverse to Kentallon Bay, continue past the grassy gully along the ridge now swinging NW. For about a mile, the interesting rock strata has created a broad and complicated ridge with innumerable small knolls holding lochan filled depressions. Frequent traces of path aid progress though the area could be very confusing in mist. Beinn a' Bheithir is an interesting mountain in itself and the combination of deep glacial valleys, complex knobbly ridges, pinnacles and cliffs are well appreciated from this route of descent.

About half a mile south west of Creag Ghorm, the true end of the horseshoe, descend westward following one of the many streams, towards the old pier one mile north of Kentallon. The slopes are steep but predominantly grassy and straightforward and on a fine day allow wonderful views of Loch Linnhe throughout. Keep to the left of the private house and garden just above the road opposite the pier to avoid ending up in someone's back garden!

FACT FILE

Distance: 10 miles Height gain: 4000 ft / 1220m

Time: 6 – 8 hours

Remarks: some pathless sections, good navigational skills needed in hillfog. Not advised in high winds.

Start: Ballachulish Village GR 080578 Finish: Kentallon Pier GR 014584 or road end Ballachulish House GR 047595

Public Transport: Ballachulish well served by buses from Fort William, Oban, Kinlochleven and Glasgow. Oban-Fort William bus for Kentallon to Ballachulish.

Stalking season: usually no access problems

AN EASIER ALTERNATIVE – INCHREE FALLS

A mile north of Onich, a signposted road leads to the forestry hamlet of Inchree just off the busy A82 Ballachulish to Fort William Road. From the car park, Forest

Enterprise have laid out two waymarked forest trails which include a visit to Glen Righ Falls. The Abhainn Righ plunges some 150 feet in an entrancing staircase of 8 falls surrounded by densely wooded banks. The third fall is the most imposing, tumbling some 50 feet. After heavy rain, it is one of the most dramatic aquatic spectacles in Scotland. An ancient major landslip diverted the course of the river. Its original course up the Dubh Glen is now a dry valley.

The 40 minute 'Waterfall Walk' climbs gently on a well made path towards the falls with a fine view en route across Loch Linnhe to Garbh Bheinn in Ardgour. The falls are seen via a series of viewpoint platforms. After climbing some 250 feet the path turns left down an easy forest road leading back towards the car park.

An information board at the car park states that the 1 hour 20 minute 'Wade's Walk' which follows part of an old military road, rewards you with 'panoramic vistas'. In reality, this 3 mile walk misses the waterfalls and climbs for 500 feet through monotonous larch and spruce. Rapid tree growth has made the views extremely restricted and very disappointing. *A much better alternative* is to follow the waterfall path past the falls and continue to the junction with the forest road. Instead of turning left as per the marked trail, turn right and climb the road for a short distance before cutting up left onto easy moorland slopes above a small crag (the lower flanks of Beinn na Glucaig). A short climb will provide infinitely better views of Loch Linnhe and the surrounding mountains than anything the Wade path can offer.

16 THE AONACH EAGACH RIDGE

The north side of the Pass of Glencoe is formed by the imposing massive pinnacled walls and gullies of the Aonach Eagach, the *'notched ridge'.* The full traverse of its two Munros provides the most sensational outing in mainland Britain. Much of its length involves easy but exposed scrambling along a narrow ridge with almost sheer drops for several thousand feet on both sides. It is therefore not for the faint hearted and some may prefer the reassurance of a rope. The holds are good throughout but unless highly experienced, do not attempt the ridge in high wind or when the rocks underfoot are wet. Under winter conditions, it is strictly for mountaineering experts only. *Do not attempt to descend from the ridge between Am Bodach and Sgor nam Fiannaidh,* unless you are first cousin to an eagle or have a parachute – seriously! A rock climber gave me another very useful piece of advice. If in any doubt about the route, keep as close to the crest as possible.

An east to west traverse affords the easiest initial ascent and later scrambling, along with the finer views. From a parking area some 300 yards west of the roadside cottages at Allt-na-Reigh, a distinct path zigzags up a grassy shoulder alongside a steep ravine. The path then drops slightly to avoid some crags before rising steeply but indistinctly on the far side. Head NW to reach the main ridge around 800 m/ 2625 ft. The steep ridge is then followed SW to the summit of Am Bodach (am botach) over a series of false tops. Alternatively, once the main path begins to swing round beside the Allt Reigh about the 450m mark, one can take to

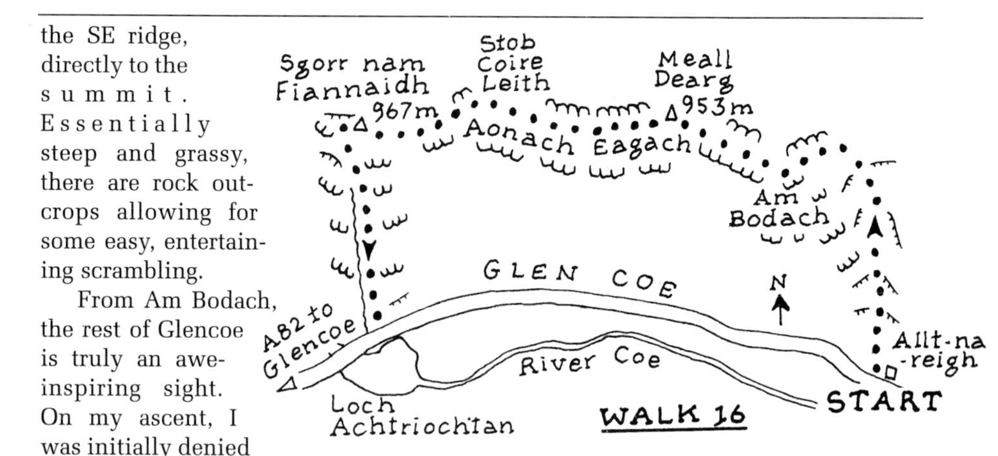

the SE ridge, directly to the summit. Essentially steep and grassy, there are rock outcrops allowing for some easy, entertaining scrambling.

From Am Bodach, the rest of Glencoe is truly an awe-inspiring sight. On my ascent, I was initially denied the fine view north to the Mamores by some curious cloud antics. Like some nebulous 'hoki - koki', the mass of cloud was repeatedly sweeping in southwards, hitting the crest of the ridge then curling back up and retreating northward. A phenomenon I've only experienced on one other mountain.

Leaving the summit WNW, the scrambling soon begins with an exposed 70ft descent of a rocky staircase, initially on the north side of the ridge before swinging round onto the crest. Straightforward walking along a very narrow airy arete leads towards the first Munro, Meall Dearg, 3118 ft / 953 m. (Pron: myowl jerrrak). Passing above near vertical gullies and cliffs plunging down to the road, the going is spectacular in the extreme. *'Red hill'* is so named because of the pink porphyrite rock which has intruded into the darker volcanic lavas which make up the rest of the ridge.

Beyond the flat topped summit, the real excitement begins, as you continuously scramble your way along very exposed narrow aretes and negotiate short gullies, chimneys, pinnacles and rocky knobs. Approaching the final main pinnacle, the crest appears an impossible scramble above a big drop, whilst to your right is a mud 'path' heading down. This is a notorious accident black spot. The apparent and inviting 'escape route' is actually very slippery and dangerous and one should keep to the rocky crest. First impressions are deceptive. The scrambling is actually easy on big 'jug' holds, though few will want to look very far down at this point!

Beyond the pinnacles, the technical difficulties cease. The ridge is level for a short while before descending to a narrow col. A path wends up steeply through the quartzite to the summit of the minor Top, Stob Coire Leith. An easy walk leads to the second Munro and a fine view back along the 'notched ridge' and Loch Leven. Sgor nam Fiannaidh 3173 ft / 967 m. (skor nan feeanee) is *'the peak of the Fian warriors'*, named after followers of the legendary Celt, Finn MacCool.

Whichever route you choose to descend, the gradients are very steep plunging 3000 feet in about a mile. The descent of the west bank of the Clachaig Gully was once very popular but is not recommended. The path is very eroded and slippery and its' start is not obvious from above. It is far safer to go a little west from the summit of Sgor nam Fiannaidh then turn due south, aiming for Loch Achtriochan.

Some 800 feet of scree, earth and boulders give way to unrelentingly steep grass. (A much longer but gentler descent can be made by continuing along the ridge to the col under the Pap of Glencoe and picking up the path which leads down to the forest edge 0.5 mile SW of Glencoe Village).

From Loch Achtriochan, it is 2.25 miles back up the glen to the car park; a chance to really appreciate the surrounding awesome mass of plunging cliffs and precipitous gullies and streams. For the last mile, a track can be followed below the road.

FACT FILE

Distance: 8 miles Height gain: 3000 ft / 914 m
Time: 6 – 8 hours in good conditions
Start / Finish: near Allt-na-Reigh A82 Glencoe GR 174566 OS Sheet 41
Remarks: very exposed narrow ridges, Grade 2 scrambling, strictly for experts in high winds and under snow.
Stalking season: unrestricted access, National Trust property
Public Transport: Buses from Edinburgh, Glasgow and Fort William pass through Glencoe.

EASY ALTERNATIVE – GLENCOE VILLAGE & HOSPITAL LOCHAN

This is an easy walk on good paths laid out around one of the most beautiful small lochans in Scotland. In early summer when the abundant rhododendrons are flowering or when the trees are decked in autumnal splendour, the views are truly stunning. Boots are not essential although the path can be a little muddy in places after heavy rain.

From the car park at the south west corner of Glencoe Village, turn right and head along the single street, past the folk museum. Dominated by the conical Pap of Glencoe, this street was once part of the main road through the glen, built in 1786.

Just before the old stone bridge, turn right. Steps on the right lead to the monument cross built in 1883 in memory of the Macdonalds who perished in the Glencoe Massacre in 1692. The name Macdonald is synonymous with the glen. The last Macdonald Laird died in 1894, ending some 500 years of the clan's domination of the area.

Returning to the main road, cross the bridge and in 50 yards turn left between gateposts up the tarmac hospital road. At a fork bear right along the track which passes the lochan public car park. The Forestry Commission has laid out 3 clearly marked paths. For those looking for just a short flat walk, then the Lochan Trail encircling the lochan is ideal. A delightful mix of spruce, pine and larch and lush deciduous woodland fronted by an extravagance of rhododendrons, frame the surrounding mountains beautifully. The artificial lochan was the brain-child of Lord Strathcona in the 1890s. He had emigrated to Canada as a young man and become head of a syndicate which built the Canadian Pacific Railway. Returning to Scotland with his half native Indian wife, he attempted to recreate his own little piece of Canada. However, they later returned to British Columbia leaving behind this scenic gem.

The longer walking option turns left just before the lochan, onto the Woodland

Trail. Twenty years ago there were a number of fine viewpoints en route through the woods. The trees have since grown up limiting the vistas somewhat but it is nonetheless a very pleasant arboreal experience, including stands of California redwoods and Lawson's cypress. On reaching the lochan, turn left and follow its shore round to the start of the third trail. A short but quite steep climb brings charming views towards Loch Leven. The track beyond, drops steeply to the lochan car park and the outward route which is reversed back into the village.
Distance: 3.5 miles Height gain: 230 ft / 70 m (2 miles for Lochan Trail only, virtually flat).
Time: 1.5 – 2 hours.

17 ASCENT OF GARBH BHEINN (LOCH LEVEN) 867m / 2846ft

Not to be confused with the Garbh Bheinn (garven) in Ardgour, this *'rough hill'* is a grand Corbett unjustly neglected by many walkers, being in close proximity to the higher and better known peaks of Glencoe. However, unlike its near neighbour, the Aonach Eagach ridge, it is a 'hands in pocket' walk within the scope of all hillwalkers, although starting from virtually sea level, every foot has to be earned. The northern slopes are quite precipitous with great drapes of scree and crag. The encompassing arms of the west and north east ridges however, offer fairly steep though straightforward routes in clear conditions.

Start from Caolasnacon on the south side of Loch Leven. There is parking in two small lay-bys close to the road bridge over the Allt Gleann a'Chaolais. Follow the obvious path above the east bank of this river for approximately 0.75 mile, then head northward up steep grassy slopes to reach the first col on the west ridge. It is then simply a matter of following up the crest of the ridge. Traces of path lead through grass, heather and bracken, wending between occasional small outcrops. Higher up, the ridge becomes better defined and stonier. Whilst walking alone, approaching a small dip in the ridge, not far from the summit, I inadvertently disturbed a male golden eagle not fifty feet away. Imperiously, it took off with a sweep

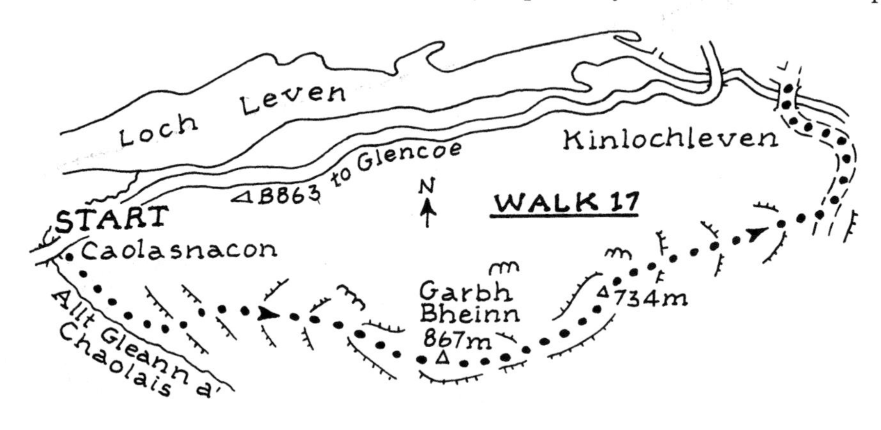

of its majestic plaid like wings, wheeling off right in front of me. The best close encounter I have had in 20 years on the Scottish hills with this magnificent creature. I cannot promise you an eagle, but on a fine day I can almost guarantee you peace and quiet and fine panoramic views along Loch Leven to Ardgour, Ben Nevis frowning over the full length of the Mamores, the bleak expanse of the Blackwater Reservoir and a little seen close up of the northern face of the pinnacled turrets of the Aonach Eagach ridge. The first of two cairns is the true summit but it is worth visiting the second, for the superior view to north and east. The tiny houses down in Kinlochleven look like Toy Town. Their gaily painted outer walls and red rooves in defence of the long winter months when the bulk of Garbh Bheinn denies the town direct sunlight.

To return, retrace your steps or head down the relatively easy slopes NW to a point at 734m. Beyond, continue descending more steeply ENE, to pick up a track low down which is the access road above the Allt Coire Mhorair, serving Kinlochleven's water reservoir. The track leads down into the town, 3 miles along the road from your start point (a bus route).

FACT FILE

Distance: west ridge only, 4 miles (the full traverse is 8 miles) Height gain: 850m / 2790 ft

Time: 4 – 5 hours

Start/Finish: Caolasnacon, Loch Leven, GR144607 OS Sheet 41

Remarks: due to absence of a clear path, good navigational skills required in hill-fog. No undue difficulties in winter conditions for those competent with ice axe and crampons.

Stalking season contact Alcan Highland Estates c/o West Highland Estates 01397 702433 or stalker 01397 702433.

Public Transport: regular buses from Fort William serve Kinlochleven via Ballachulish. From Oban, change at Ballachulish

18 ASCENT OF MAM NA GUALAINN 796 m / 2611 ft

This Corbett nestles on the north side of Loch Leven, somewhat dwarfed by the neighbouring Mamores Munros to the north, of which it is really a southern outlier. This fact along with its shape gives rise to its name, *'the pass of the shoulder'*, (maam na goouleen). Inspite of its relatively lowly position, it is a grandiose viewpoint for Loch Leven and the surrounding peaks. With the exception of one short steep section, gradients underfoot are moderate and the going predominantly grassy, making for a very pleasant half day outing.

On the north shore of Loch Leven, a signposted path a quarter of a mile east of Callert House, heads NNE towards the Lairigmor, part of the old military road to Fort William. *(There is parking just to the east of the start, and to the west of the house)*. Initially the path meanders through a birch and oak wood. Once onto open ground, the path through the grass and bracken is not always clear. If you should lose the way, one can soon pick it up again on higher ground where it becomes better defined though often somewhat muddy. Your only companions are likely to be

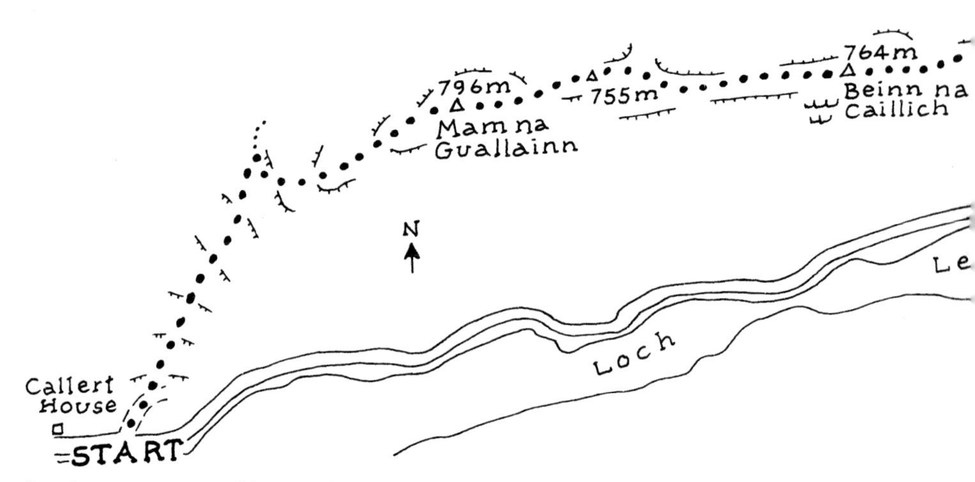

the sheep, pipits and buzzards and if in late spring, the cuckoo. On my visit however, motorcycles had churned up the mud into a morass for a short distance. I did not appreciate this intrusion by modern machines, although the pall bearers who used to carry coffins down here, may have been glad of a helping hand. The path is an old coffin route, the hearses being ferried from Callert to the tiny isle of Eilean Munde, named after Mun, a Celtic saint. For many centuries this was the burial place of the Camerons of Callert and the Macdonalds of Glencoe. Callert itself has a grim history. Almost its entire population died of the plague some 200 hundred years ago when a Swedish ship carrying the disease, anchored there.

On a brighter note, the route cuts a swaithe through a mass of flowers; heath milkwort, tormentil, lousewort, oxalis and orchids to name but a few. Even in drought conditions, the river cascading down the valley remains lively. Whilst behind you, there are splendid views across the farmland, woodland and Loch Leven to the cliff girt Glencoe peaks and Beinn a'Bheithir.

Approaching the col, abandon the path and head up the broad WSW ridge on moderate slopes of grass and mossy heath which lead to a stony summit.

Having savoured the fine summit vistas, retrace your steps back to Callert. Alternatively, if in a two car party or a keen cyclist, a linear traverse is possible, continuing eastward along a further 1.5 miles of easy ridge to Beinn na Caillich. From here, a path cuts steeply down the east ridge and crosses the Allt Nathrach to join the West Highland Way track which can be followed down to the eastern end of Loch Leven.

FACT FILE

Distance: 5 miles Height gain: 2630 ft / 800m (longer optional traverse 8 miles, 3130 ft / 953m)

Time: 3 – 4 hours (4.5 – 6 hours longer traverse)

Remarks: No undue difficulties under winter conditions and straightforward navigation in mist.

Start / Finish: Callert on B863, GR 094603. (Finish longer traverse GR 175623) OS Sheet 41
Public Transport – none on the north shore of Loch Leven
Stalking – Alcan Highland Estate c/o West High Estates office Tel. 01397 702433 or stalker Tel. 01855 831337

EASIER ALTERNATIVES

18A RIVER LEVEN FALLS

The environs of Kinlochleven is blessed with a number of accessible fine waterfalls which make for attractive and enjoyable walks whatever the weather. The energetic may wish to take the path right up the River Leven to the Blackwater Reservoir, built by some 3000 navvies in the first decade of the century, to supply water to the aluminium works. One cannot help but notice the huge pipelines hugging the sides of the valley. The River Leven and its tributaries, cascade down a series of falls. Fortunately, the most spectacular of these are just over a mile from town.

The main road through Kinlochleven passes the Tailrace Inn near a cluster of 3 churches. Across the road from here, follow the West Highland Way signs along a tarmac path beside the river. The outflow of water from the power station provides an interesting spectacle. Turn right onto Wade's Road and follow to a track leading towards a bridge over the River Leven. Just before this bridge, fork left up a path signed, *'Ciaran Path and Dam'*, which rises above the river through delightful oak and birch woodland. There are some pleasing glimpses to the surrounding mountains and in winter with the absence of foliage, to the raging River Leven with its numerous falls. The going underfoot is a bit rough and stony and after rain can be very wet, though not muddy. Having climbed about 400 feet in a mile and crossed 4 minor burns, the path crosses a bridge over the Allt na' h-Eilde. Some 200 yards beyond on the left, a notable fall thunders down this tributary stream; a fine spectacle after heavy rain. Return by your outward route.

Above the aluminium works, there is an impressive double fall (MacKay's Fall) plunging some 20 feet through a fine rocky gorge. Just beyond the start of the "Ciaran Path,'take a rough and usually wet path beside the north bank of the river. In quarter of a mile it reaches the gorge. The route continues rather awkwardly above the gorge, weaving thorough small trees and occasionally clambering up wee quartz slabs.

Distance to both falls, 3.5 miles, height gain 400 feet (to Blackwater Reservoir 7.5 miles)

Public Transport: regular buses from Fort William to Kinlochleven via Ballachulish. From Oban, change at Ballachulish

18B GREY MARE'S FALL & LOCH EILDE MOR

More easily accessible, the spectacular Grey Mare's Fall is just a short walk from the houses on the north side of Kinlochleven. The Allt Coire na Ba thunders down

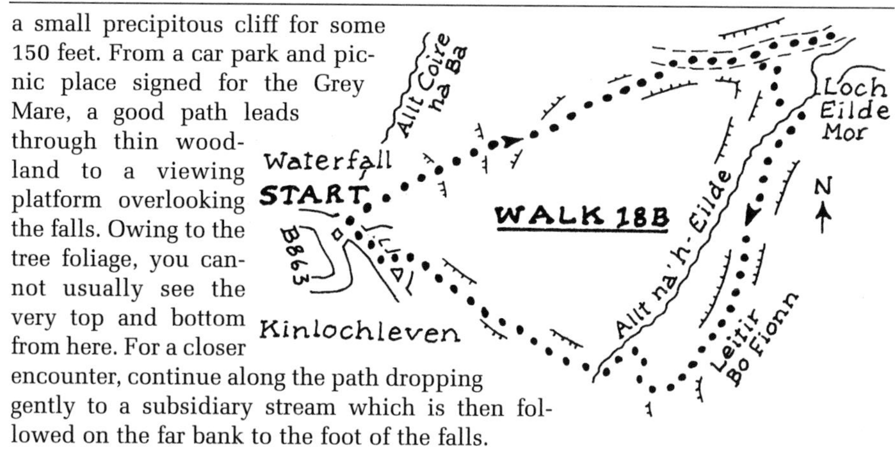

a small precipitous cliff for some 150 feet. From a car park and picnic place signed for the Grey Mare, a good path leads through thin woodland to a viewing platform overlooking the falls. Owing to the tree foliage, you cannot usually see the very top and bottom from here. For a closer encounter, continue along the path dropping gently to a subsidiary stream which is then followed on the far bank to the foot of the falls.

Stronger walkers desiring a half day walk with superb and varied views, will want to turn (NE) uphill away from the falls and take the path leading to Loch Eilde Mor amidst wild moorland beneath the mighty Mamores ridge. From the viewing platform, continue gently uphill on a path which soon joins the main track. In another 100 yards at a path junction, bear slightly left over a burn and take the track on the far side leading steeply uphill through beautiful birch and rowan woodland. In September when the rowan is in fruit and leaves are hinting of autumn, the route is particularly entrancing. As height is gained, your labours are rewarded with a classic picture postcard view down the full length of the fjord like Loch Leven; the Pap of Glencoe and Beinn na Caillich standing sentinel on either side. Once clear of the woods, the gradient eases considerably as the track cuts directly across the grassy and heathery moorland. On reaching a land Rover track, turn right and follow gently downhill to Loch Eilde Mor. This can be a desolate place in bad weather but in the right conditions when the surrounding rounded hills are reflected in the still waters, it can be an enchanting place. This is especially true when the heather and ling are in bloom or under winter conditions. A boat is often moored away from the boathouse lending foreground to your photographs.

There are a number of return options. You can retrace your steps but the steep section of the path which is bearable in ascent, is an abomination in descent; the stones being too big underfoot for comfort. One alternative is to keep on the Land Rover track rather than turn off on the route of ascent. Just as the track begins to swing NW up the valley of the Allt coire na Ba, a path turns down to your left and heads back down into the town near the Grey Mare. The going is often steep and can be very slippery during snow melt or after heavy rain.

The more interesting alternative allows you to combine this walk with the aforementioned River Leven walk. From the boatshed, return along the track for about quarter of a mile. A path branches off to the left, leading to a dam at the start of the Allt na h-Eilde. The path descends for 1.5 miles near a pipe line above the river, to a viewpoint at Leitir Bo Fionn. Turn right at a path junction (GR 210613) and head steeply down to the path along the River Leven. This is followed back

into town as per previous walk.
Distance: 6 miles Height gain: 1150 ft / 350 m (Grey Mare only 0.5 mile)
Time: 3 – 4 hours
Start / Finish: Grey Mare car park, Kinlochleven GR 187624 OS Sheet 41
Public Transport: Buses run from Fort William to Kinlochleven via Ballachulish.

19 ASCENT OF BROWN COW HILL 942ft / 287m & GLEN NEVIS FOREST TRAILS

Although rather a shapeless moorland hill rising sharply above Fort William, this short ascent affords fine views of lower Glen Nevis, part of the Great Glen and Lochs Linnhe and Eil beyond the town. For the less energetic or in poorer weather, some easy forest trails are also available in the locality.

Park at the 'Roaring Mill' layby (GR 121740), some thousand yards above the Bridge of Nevis near the entrance to Glen Nevis. Take a few minutes to visit the water sculptured rocky banks and the low set of falls straddling the Water of Nevis; a noisy aquatic spectacle after rain, hence its name. Follow the road south into the glen for several hundred yards before bearing right onto a forest track signed 'Braveheart Car Park'. This was constructed during the location filming of the cinema hit and offers alternative parking to Roaring Mill (though note it has a 6' 6'height restriction).
Carry on past following the gentle graded red waymarked 'Wishing Stone Walk'. At present the trees are short enough to allow some fine views to the peaks of Sgurr a' Mhaim and Stob Ban rising impressively above the southern end of Glen Nevis and to the mighty bulk of Ben Nevis across the glen, brooding like a beached whale. In a thousand yards turn right up the signed 'Peat Track'. The path is well constructed, though climbs steeply for a time through the thin mixed forest. Go through a gate at a fence just beyond the top of the tree line and cut across 400 yards of rough moorland to gain the stony road which services the communications mast on the summit of Brown Cow Hill. Having enjoyed the aerial views over the town and lochs, retrace your steps to the foot of the 'Peat Track' (or continue down it towards Achintore near Fort William). Now follow the remainder of the 'Wishing Stone Walk', turning gently down the hill past the ancient burial ground of the MacSorlie Camerons of Glen Nevis, a clan sadly no more. Turn left at the road and follow the pavement back to the start. You pass the large 'Wishing' or "Council Stone' (Clach Shomhairle). Legend has it that you can make a wish which will come true – if you see the stone move!
In addition to the easy 1.25 miles Wishing Stone Walk, the waymarked 6 miles Dun Deardail Walk begins at the 'Braveheart' car park. This climbs up moderate forest

roads and paths to the top of the forest where lie the vitrified stone ramparts of an iron age fort. This affords grand views across and along Glen Nevis.
Four miles further down the glen near the Falls of Polldubh, the waymarked 2.5 miles Achriabhach Forest Walk offers a short but often steep walk which for part of the way follows the Achriabhach Burn: spectacular in spate.
Brown Cow Hill Distance: 4.5 miles Height gain: 900ft/ 274m Time: 2 hours.

20 THE STEALL HORSESHOE

Glen Nevis is considered one of the loveliest valleys in the Highlands. Stretching for 9 miles along the south side of the glen, is a chain of 11 shapely Munros, the Mamores, linked by narrow ridges, rimming a succession of deeply carved corries. Although this walk ascends five of these Munros, there are no great drops between them and you will expend no more energy than in climbing neighbouring Ben Nevis on its own. The route is also far more interesting than slogging up the 'Ben' and is less likely to be cloud capped. The first section of the walk to Steall is easy and very beautiful; a must for everyone, including the casual stroller.

From the car park at the road end in Glen Nevis, take the clearly defined path signed for 'Corrour Station', beneath the dramatic water slides on the precipitous slabby flanks of Ben Nevis. It heads eastward through a spectacular and awesome, deep, rocky gorge, through which the River Nevis roars, losing 400 feet of height in a mile. Passing through delightful woodland of pine, rowan, oak and birch, the path threads a way between rocky bluffs, climbing quite gently. The path suddenly emerges between the cliffs, into a flat, grassy meadow, dominated by a glacial hanging valley, from which pours the magnificent 347 foot An Steall Ban waterfall *(the white spout)*, tumbling over great grey slabs. Even in relative drought conditions, it cannot fail to impress.

The route onto the Mamores requires a sense of adventure, crossing over the River Nevis about 600 yards before Steall falls. The 3 strand wire bridge is safer than it looks. People shorter than around 5' 4'however, may find it difficult to use. The river is usually quiet within the vicinity and providing it is not in spate, can be paddled with care or crossed on stepping stones. *(If in any doubt however, don't cross. The first 3 Munros can be climbed from Kinlochleven and the other 2 from Polldubh in Glen Nevis)*. Across the river, head towards the waterfall and pick up the excellent stalkers' path zigzagging up onto An Gearanach 982m / 3230 ft (an gyaranach) which is unnamed on most maps at GR 187670. It affords excellent views along Glen Nevis. The easily graded ridge to the minor top of An Garbhanach, includes a short, easy and entertaining scramble along a narrow, exposed arete formed by uptilted rock strata. An optional path initially to the right of the crest, avoids any difficulties. Beyond the top, an easy grassy ridge, brings the flat topped dome of the second Munro, Stob Coire a'Chairn 983m / 3219 ft, *'peak of the corrie of the cairn'*.

The path continues easily down to a grassy col. The short climb onto Am

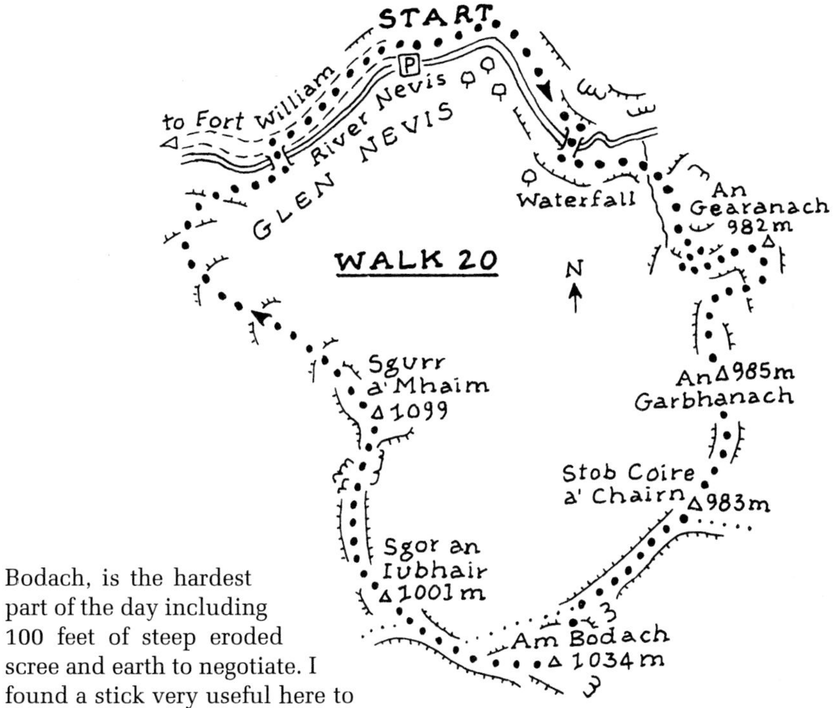

Bodach, is the hardest part of the day including 100 feet of steep eroded scree and earth to negotiate. I found a stick very useful here to give purchase to the feet. Am Bodach (am botach) 1034m / 3382ft, *'the old man'*, was named at a time when few survived to old age and the aged were greatly respected. It is a fine peak with a precipitous and rocky east face above the Coire na Ba, well seen if ascended from Kinlochleven.

An easy grassy ridge leads eastward over several small hillocks to the flat topped fourth Munro (unnamed on map),'Sgor an Iubhair 1001m / 3284ft, (skor an yooar) *'peak of the yew tree'* from where the cliff girt eastern face of Stob Ban looks very impressive.

The route now leaves the main spine of the Mamores ridge and heads northward over a minor top to the start of the 'Devil's Ridge'. This airy ridge is rather exposed for a short time and necessitates easy scrambling. The less assured may appreciate the security of a rope here. An easier way can be found just below the crest on the left. A straightforward ascent of some 400 feet brings the final Munro, Sgurr a'Mhaim, 1099m / 3601ft (pron: skoor a vaaeem) 'peak of the large rounded hill', with its distinctive white quartzite capping. From the cairn, a grandiose view opens out, along the whole of Glen Nevis with its large attendant array of Munros and countless hills to the west.

The long NW shoulder of the mountain, offers a straightforward descent into Glen Nevis. An initial 800 feet of scree, gives way to steep grass and an increasingly distinct path, zigzagging down towards Achriabhach and the Falls of Polldubh. Near to the foot of the descent, abandon the path and head NE down tufted grass to eventually join a path that closely follows the south bank of the Water of Nevis. Some 0.75 mile from the car park, cross the footbridge and follow the road back to your start point.

FACT FILE

Distance: 11 miles Height gain: 4400ft / 1340m
Time: 6 – 8 hours
Start/Finish: road end Glen Nevis GR 167691 OS Sheet 41
Remarks: The Devil's Ridge and ridge between An Gearanach & An Garbhanach are not recommended in very high winds or under winter conditions unless very experienced.
Stalking season: contact The Stalker, Alcan Highland Estates Tel. 01855 831337

AN EASY ALTERNATIVE

The first section of the main walk to the meadow within sight of An Steall Fall is a must (see text above). The path is a little rough underfoot however and strong footwear is advised. It is worthwhile continuing to Steall ruin at the confluence of the River Nevis with the Allt Coire Guibhsachan. Follow the west (left) bank of this side stream for a short way to enjoy a stunning succession of dramatic waterfalls and pools, particularly during or after heavy rain.
Distance 3.5 miles

A FEW WORDS ABOUT THE 'BEN'

Being the highest mountain in Britain, Ben Nevis entices scores of tourists from home and abroad who have never or rarely climbed any hills before, to attempt the strenuous ascent. For novices I would advise sticking to the tourist route from Achintee above Fort William; a 4400-foot slog on a badly eroded path that can be very slippery on the descent. The route is obvious, at least until the last section. The summit plateau often holds snow well into early summer. Given the treacherous cliffs and gullies close to the summit, accurate navigation is essential in hill-fog. If you are inexperienced, do not hesitate to turn back if the weather deteriorates.

The tourist route misses the finest part of the mountain; the magnificent and awesome 2000 feet northern complex of cliffs, buttresses, ridges and gullies. These can be appreciated by taking the tourist route to half way, then following the path which turns off to the left, contouring for a mile beside Lochan Meall an t-Suidhe into the valley of the Allt a Mhuillinn and follows it up beneath the cliffs. Retrace your steps from the Charles Inglis Clark Memorial Hut. For experienced walkers, this is the finest way to ascend Ben Nevis (with the exception of including a traverse of the Carn Mor Dearg arete) provided the upper valley is not choked with snow and ice. The route continues past the hut, then scrambles up a boulder staircase to the col between Carn Mor Dearg and Ben Nevis. A faint path then leads up through another boulder field to the summit.

Oban Bay by Dunollie *Walk 6*

Mull from Ben Cruachan *Walk 7*

Pap of Glencoe from Hospital Lochan *Walk 16*

Carsaig Arches, Mull *Walk 23*

Iona Abbey with the Paps of Jura beyond *Walk 24*

Puffins on Lunga *Walk 25*

Rois-bheinn & An Stac *Walk 49*

Eigg & Rum from the Mallaig road *Walk 53*

21 ASCENT OF DUN DA GHAOITHE 766m / 2514 ft

'The fort of the two winds', (doon da goeya) is well seen from the Oban ferry as you approach Craignure, rising majestically above Duart Castle. It is one of the finest viewpoints in Mull and has the added attraction of being very accessible for foot passengers arriving from Oban on a day trip.

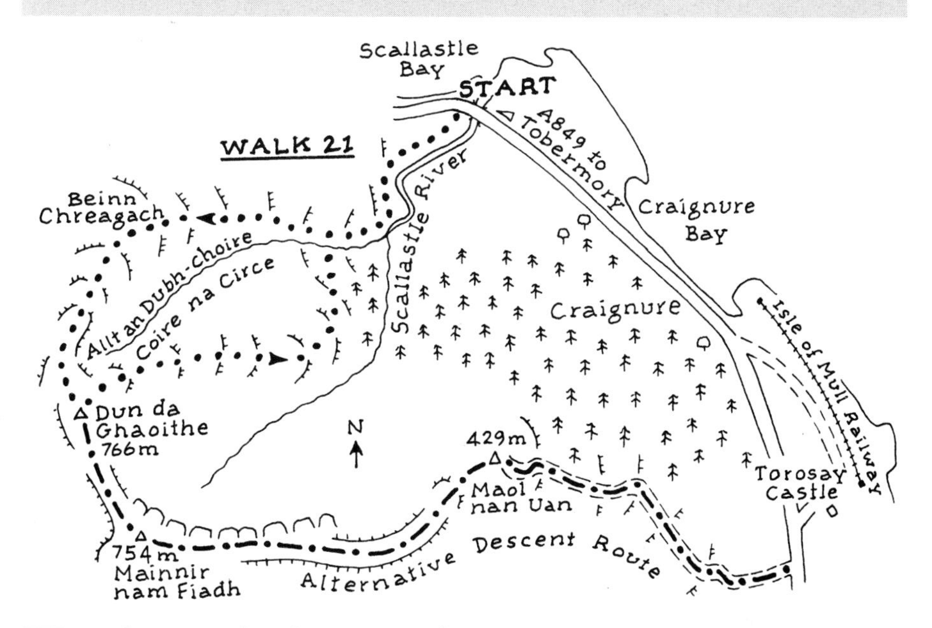

Tree plantations bar direct access from Craignure. Either take a bus or walk along the A849 Tobermory road NW for 1.25 miles to Scallastle. About a quarter of a mile beyond the road bridge over the Scallastle River, leave the road and head SW over the moorland rising above the north bank of the Allt an Dubh-choire which cascades in an attractive series of small falls and pools. Continue on to the broad easy ridge of Beinn Creagach, which swings round the head of Coire na Circe to reach the summit of Dun da Ghaoithe. The going is pathless but essentially grassy up to the stonier upper slopes and is straightforward in clear conditions. From the large summit cairn, there are grand views to the hills of Argyll and Morvern over the Firth of Lorn and Sound of Mull respectfully and to innumerable islands.

To vary the descent, one can head down the east ridge to the top of the tree line. The forest edge is then followed northward back to the Allt an Dubh-choire. Cross the river and aim back to your starting point at Scallastle.

Alternatively, if you wish to include a visit to the interesting medieval MacLean stronghold of Duart Castle (open May – Oct.) or to the 19th century Torosay Castle with its attractive gardens and fine statues (open mid April – mid October), then head SE along a gentle ridge to Mainnir nam Fiadh 754 metres. At the peak turn east and head down to the TV mast on Maol nan Uan. A rough service road then zigzags down to the main road, 1.5 miles south of Craignure. Rather than follow the road back, you can catch the miniature train from Torosay Castle or walk along an adjacent track. Fionnphort – Craignure buses also pass here upto 3 times daily.

FACT FILE

Distance: 8.5 miles (if descending via Maol nan Uan 10 miles) Height gain 2514 ft/ 766 m
Time: 5 – 7 hours
Start/ Finish: Craignure Pier GR 718372 OS Sheet 49
Remarks: being pathless, good navigational skills needed in hillfog
Stalking season: Sept – Feb. contact Torosay estate office Craignure Tel. 01680 812421
Public Transport: Cal. Mac. Ferries Oban – Craignure: Tel 01631 562285. Buses pass Scallastle & Torosay

AN EASY ALTERNATIVE

For an easy stroll, one can follow the shore south of Craignure, round the Minister's Point then continue on the track to Torosay. This affords excellent views of the Morvern hills beyond the Sound of Mull.

22 ASCENT OF BEN MORE 966m / 3169 ft

Ben More *(correctly Beinn Mhor)* simply means 'big hill', being the largest mountain on the island of Mull. It is a majestic peak of character, the culminating point of three ridges, dominating the western hills. The narrow eastern arete offers the most exhilarating ascent, allowing for easy, entertaining though optional scrambling. Try and save for a fine day. Not only is Ben More a superb viewpoint but the summit is composed of magnetic volcanic rocks, the highest accumulation of Tertiary lavas in Britain. A compass is therefore useless here and will make navigation tricky in hillfog; undesirable given the broken north eastern and south eastern cliffs, lying in wait for the unwary.

Beside Loch na Keal, on the B8035, 7-miles south west of Salen, there is ample parking on roadside grass, beside the bridge over the Abhainn na h-Uamha. A moderately graded stalkers' path follows the west bank of this delightful river. It has carved down through the layers of ancient lava to form a fme, deep, narrow gorge, adorned with oak and rowan trees. Attractive waterfalls abound along the river, although after a prolonged drought, become somewhat ragged and thin. As height is gained, an impressive array of islands and the precipitous cliffs of nearby Creag Mhor show to the west. Gleann na Beinne Fada is essentially grassy and the peaty path is inclined to be wet. By way of compensation, a profusion of pretty bog loving plants thrive here.

The path does not go up to the desired col east of A'Choich and in the upper reaches of the glen you must abandon it and take the easy, grassy slopes leading to the pass. The impressive ridge climbing to A'Choich, is narrow and increasingly rocky. If so inclined, there are optional wee entertaining scrambles en route above the straightforward path. The subsidiary top of A'Choich (a cheech) *"the breast"*, tapers to a sharp point. This craggy environment is golden eagle territory. They often nest on the nearby crags of Creag na h-Iolaire. From A'Choich's stony summit, the, steep and airy east ridge of Ben More, appears rather formidable, especially when thin clouds are swirling around enhancing the precipitous corries. In such conditions, the central hills of Mull, smoke like the volcanoes they once were many millions of years ago.

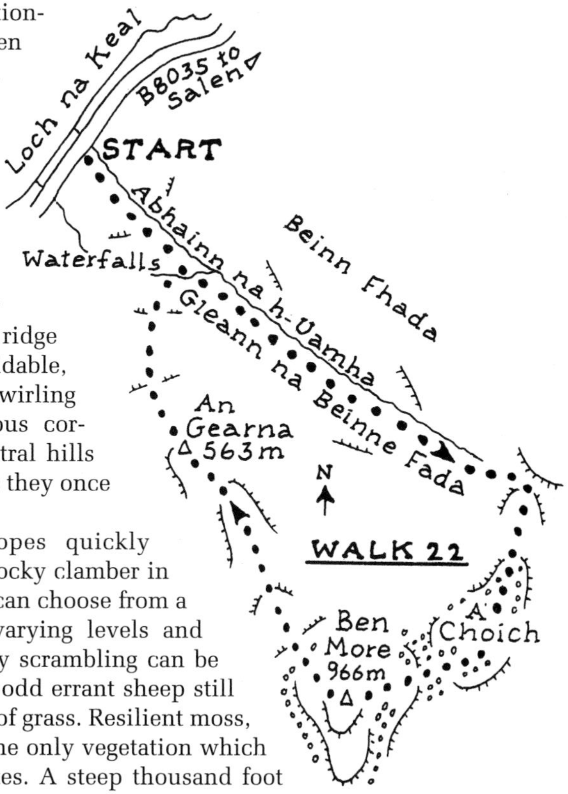

Leaving A'Chioch, the slopes quickly steepen and the path is an easy rocky clamber in places. Beyond the next col, one can choose from a number of enjoyable paths at varying levels and degrees of difficulties. Any tricky scrambling can be easily avoided if so desired. The odd errant sheep still grazes here inspite of an absence of grass. Resilient moss, lady's mantle and eyebright are the only vegetation which seem to thrive in the rocky wastes. A steep thousand foot climb brings the summit and if you are fortunate, a wonderful panorama of much of Mull, the Argyllshire hills and a glittering array of islands including Rhum and Skye.

The easiest line of descent (and for anyone with a poor head for heights, the safest line of ascent) is down the broad NW ridge. This ridge splits into two high up. In clear conditions, it is easy to keep to the right hand arm, on the north side of a shallow hollow formed by the Abhainn Dhiseig. From An Gearna, a very steep grassy descent leads back to the path beside the Abhainn na h-Uamha and the route of ascent. If caught in mist at the summit, given the uselessness of a compass, the cairned path seemingly leading down the NW ridge, can cause confusion. The path leads down the left hand arm of the ridge and finishes at Dhiseig, a mile along the road from your start point. If the fog does not descend too far, it is possible to follow the path until out of the mist, then cut across the shallow hollow to join the An Gearna ridge.

FACT FILE

Distance: 8 miles Height gain: 3500 ft / 1066m

Time: 5 - 7 hours

Start & Finish: B8035 by Loch na Keal GR 507368 OS Sheet 47 or 48

Remarks: The east ridge not recommended in strong gales or under winter condi-

tions unless highly experienced. Good map skills essential in hillfog.
Stalking season: contact Benmore Estate c/o West Highland Estates, Oban Tel 01631 563617
or Knock House 01680 300356
No public transport beyond Salen

EASIER ALTERNATIVES
It is worthwhile following the first 1.5 miles of the above route along Gleann na Beinn Fada, given the scenic and floral interest.

Alternatively, park at Knock, 3 miles to the north east (4 miles SW of Salen). From here, an ancient right of way follows the western shore of Loch Ba. A gentle track extends right along the partially wooded loch into Glen Cannel, at the head of which stands Beinn Chaisgidle. Of interest to geomorphologists and geologists, this peak is part of the eroded remnants of huge volcanic explosions here some 60 million years ago, which laid down huge lava beds and left a huge granite ring-dyke five miles in diameter and some 300 feet thick, centred on Loch Ba.

23 CARSAIG ARCHES – MULL

The Isle of Mull is not only blessed with a fine range of mountains, it also boasts a superb coastline, particularly along its southern fringes. This walk takes you from flower carpeted moorland to wild cliffs, culminating in the spectacular sight of Carsaig Arches. Lovers of boulder scrambling are in for a treat along the surprisingly rough coast, where boots are essential and crowds non existent. *It is important to check the tide tables before setting out to avoid full high tide.*

The walk begins on the A849 Craignure – Fionnphort road 5.5 miles east of Bunessan. On the west side of the road bridge at Traigh nam Beach, a forestry track with limited parking at its start, passes a bungalow and winds gently uphill above Beach River, bordered by a colourful variety of bog loving plants. In good weather, Ben More and the lesser hills of Mull will hove into view across Loch Scridain, although Ben More is notorious for keeping its woolly hat pulled well down, even when all about it is clear.

A mile on, just before a locked gate, the Abhainn an Easa Mhoir flows over the track and tumbles down in an attractive waterfall. It shouldn't be a problem, though may involve a wee paddle if the stones are covered.

The excellent track heads across the Brolas plateau, now heavily afforested in young firs. Flowers continue to be abundant including orchids, ragwort, cross leaved heath, bell heather, self heal and stichwort. The Land-Rover track gives way to a narrower, grassy track leading southward. Once across a stile, a sheep track heads down to the ruined cottages at Airigh Mhic Cribhain. Above and to your left lies the lofty pointed prow of Cadha an da Luain. A small remnant of the highest lava flow in the island, it now tilts landwards, capping the high cliffs.

From the cottages, aim south westward. A path battles its way through thick bracken to reach the cliff top at GR476196, just to the left of the lowest point, where a burn disappears in a waterfall over the cliffs. Try and avoid the deep boggy holes as you descend to the cliff edge. I ended up with a bootful of cold, peaty water!

About 100 metres to the west of the waterfall, a steeply, shelving, grassy gully, provides the only safe way down to the beach. Traces of path ease progress. Near the gully, is a wonderfully sheltered nook, ideal for lunch, just above the sea and surrounded by clumps of bonny sea campion. The setting is quite spectacular with Atlantic breakers crashing against the bouldery shore, overlooked by the towering vertical cliffs upto 800 feet high, patrolled by wheeling gannets.

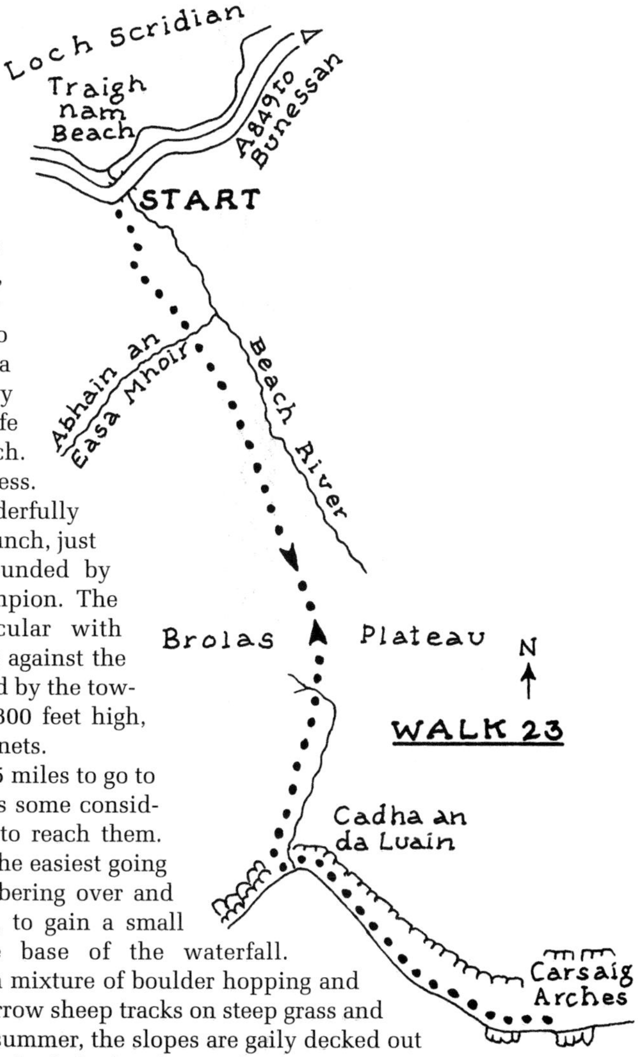

There is only some 1.5 miles to go to Carsaig Arches but it takes some considerable time and exertion to reach them. Initially, the beach offers the easiest going and fun can be had clambering over and round the huge boulders, to gain a small stony cove beyond the base of the waterfall. Thereafter is slow going; a mixture of boulder hopping and scrambling or taking to narrow sheep tracks on steep grass and scree above the beach. In summer, the slopes are gaily decked out in birdsfoot trefoil, thyme, thrift, herb Robert and stonecrop.

The arches are hidden from sight until the last 1/4 mile. From a distance, they are dwarfed by some of the tallest cliffs in Britain, but on closer inspection reveal spectacular edifices. The first arch with a curious 'chimney' rock on top, is the tallest and narrowest. At high tide the sea surges through the keyhole shaped arch. The second arch, in complete contrast, is much squatter with a lower, wider span which forms a tremendous wind tunnel one can walk through. It appears to be made of basaltic columns; rather like The Giant's Causeway on stilts.

Most walkers will have to retrace their steps. Two car parties however have the option of continuing eastward along the coast to Carsaig hamlet. A steep grassy climb beside the second arch, gives access to the rough, rolling clifftops heading north eastward. Close to the Nun's Pass, a steep grassy break in the cliffs, gives access to the shore which can then be followed.

FACT FILE
Distance: 10 miles Height gain: 500 ft/152m
Time: 5 – 6 hours
Start /Finish: GR 465242 on A849. Alternative finish at Carsaig GR 544218 OS Sheet 48
Remarks: Avoid high tide unless you are a very experienced climber
Public transport: Craignure – Fionnphort buses pass start upto 3 times daily
EASIER OPTION
The first section of the main walk is within the capabilities of most people. The going as far as the ruined cottages at Airigh Mhic Cribhain is very gentle with little height gain and provides plenty of scenic and floral interest.
Distance 6 miles

24 IN THE STEPS OF COLUMBA -- THE ROUND OF IONA

The Isle of Iona lies off the western tip of Mull and is often visited on a day trip from Oban but this gives you barely one to two hours to explore. With its delightful coastline, breathtaking sea views and fascinating historical buildings, this small enchanting island deserves more attention. This walk samples the best of Iona. Don't rush, there is so much that is worthwhile to absorb.

After arriving at the ferry jetty from Mull, take the road southward along Martyr's Bay. The cove is so named because of a Viking massacre of sixty eight monks in 806, on one of their periodic raids on the island. Things are a little more peaceful nowadays however, and you are more likely to see cows quietly resting on the beach.

Beyond the road end there is no set route. Make your way towards the southern end of the island; sheep tracks are very useful. The going is grassy and initially often steep as you wend between the small crags. Eventually fairly flat, higher ground is reached. Cotton grass, bog pimpernel and bog asphodel are evident, an indication of the grounds' usually boggy state. Southward, the islands of Islay and Jura are seen to advantage.

Being covered in innumerable knolls, the ground is much more complicated than the map suggests. A compass can be useful to orientate yourself. Work your way down to the Port of the Coracle (Port na Curaich), a delightful rocky cove with a pebbled beach, strewn with a fascinating mixture of quartz, marble, feldspar, hornblende, epidote and slate. It is here supposedly, that Columba first stepped ashore from Ireland with 12 followers in 503 and started the movement that brought Christianity to Scotland. According to legend, Columba arrived on the eve of Pentecost, the symbol for which is a dove. Columba is the Latin for dove, which is Iona in Hebrew.

Once you've finished beachcombing, take the path heading north past Loch

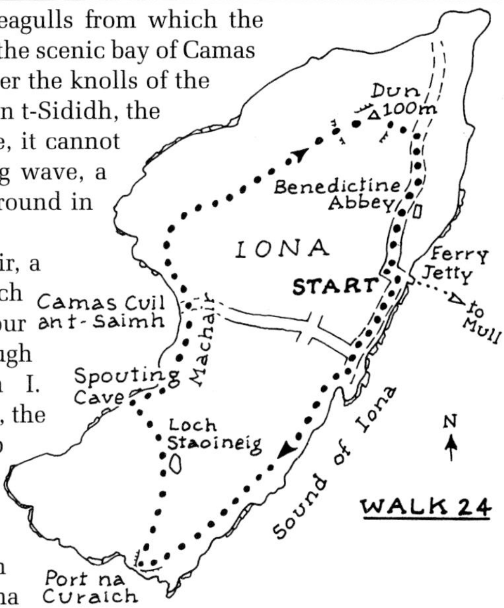

Staoineag, complete with raucous seagulls from which the name derives. Before you descend to the scenic bay of Camas Cuil an t-Saimh, detour westward over the knolls of the cliff top to get a close look at Uamh an t-Sididh, the Spouting Cave. Even from a distance, it cannot fail to impress. With every incoming wave, a fountain of water bursts above the ground in a spectacular display.

Heading north, cross the Machair, a grassy expanse beside the sea which doubles as a tiny golf course. Work your way over and round the small rough knolls and moorland onto Dun I. Although only 382 feet above the sea, the island's highest point gives superb views. The mountains of Mull, Jura and Rhum show well. Most of Iona is displayed. You can even watch the Spouting Cave in action through binoculars. The north headland of Iona is in total contrast to the rest of the island; being formed of wonderfully white, dazzling, clean shell-sand which is blown across the island each winter, fertilising the fields in the process. Seaward lie Staffa, the Treshnish Isles, Coll, Tiree and the Ardnamurchan peninsula. This summit is just the place for quiet meditation. No wonder it was so popular with Columba himself. You'll sense that Iona has a special atmosphere, all of its own.

A steep, slithery path leads down to the road, from where the Benedictine Abbey is just a few minutes away. Dating from the 13th century, it gradually fell into ruin during the 17th century, thanks to the quarrels between Charles I and the Convenanters. It was eventually restored in the 1900's. The inside is very simple but impressive, with an atmosphere you can almost touch. Outside are two beautifully carved Celtic crosses more than 1000 years old and the remains of a third.

Next door is the restored St Oran's Chapel, the island's oldest surviving building, dating from 1080. Reputedly, sixty kings are buried here, though there is no evidence of their tombs. An indication however of the island's holy standing.

En route to the jetty, pause at the ruins of a nunnery, founded in the 13th century. Inspite of only being partially restored, it is still one of the finest examples of this type of building in Britain. I can recommend the fish and chips at Grant's Restaurant, to while away any remaining time before you catch the last ferry!

FACT FILE

Distance: 7 miles Height gain: approx. 600 ft/ 183m

Time: A leisurely 4 – 6 hours

Start/Finish: Ferry jetty GR286239 OS Sheet 48

Public Transport: Regular ferries to Mull and Iona with connecting buses between Craignure and Fionnphort. Tel: CalMac: 01631 562285

EASY WALKING ON MULL & THE TRESHNISH ISLANDS

25 LUNGA & STAFFA

Along with Iona, the other islands not to be missed for their dramatic coastlines and ornithological interest are Lunga and Staffa. During the summer, day cruises run to Staffa from Fionnphort & Ulva Ferry on Mull, Iona and Oban. Gordon Grant runs trips combining both islands, from Fionnphort. Walking distances are very short but the climbing is often steep and strong footwear is recommended.

Lunga is the largest of the Treshnish Isles. A short but steep path leads from the landing area onto a grassy terrace above the lower cliffs. Within a few yards you will come across great social gathering of appealing puffins. They are seemingly unafraid of humans and will allow you close enough for great photos but be careful not to disturb them. Work your way along the narrow sheep tracks towards the cliffs of Dun Cruit, (Harp's Rock), whose outline from certain angles resembles a Celtic Harp. It comprises a dramatic cliff isolated by a deep vee shaped cleft, lashed by the Atlantic waves. It is the main bird breeding colony on the island with narrow ledges crowded with fulmars, razorbills, guillemots and kittiwakes. Under great boulders, shags nursing their young chicks make an angry hissing squawk as you pass. Masses of yellow lichen and thrift provide a colourful backcloth. Precipitous cliffs stretch along the island's coastline with the curiously shaped island of Dutchman's Cap sitting beyond. Seals can often be seen in the surrounding waters and in autumn breed here. It is well worth climbing the steep grassy slopes onto the top of the cliffs and yomping through the bracken for a couple of hundred yards towards the other side of the island, for a great view towards Staffa and Mull.

All the Treshnish Isles were once used for animal grazing. Getting the animals on and off could be very problematical for there are no jetties. On occasions, sheep were helicoptered on or off when boat landings were impossible, whilst cattle had to swim to and from the vessels. As a human it can be quite tricky returning to the boat, depending on the state of the tide. Tight skirts for the ladies are not advised as you may have to grab the rail and leap, with assistance from the boatman.

Staffa's name derives from the Norse for Island of Pillars. Cliffs of columnar basalt rise from the sea, convoluted into countless wonderful shapes. From the landing area, a short but very slippery walk over eroded basalt columns, leads to Fingal's Cave. A handrail runs for much of the way but there are gaps and it is easy to slip or trip. The cave is as awe-inspiring as Mendelssohn's famous overture. The surge of the waves echoes around the 250 foot long cavern, 70 feet high, complete with vaulted roof; an incredible natural cathedral. The froth from the waves at the entrance is sometimes thrown over 70 feet into the air.

Having returned to the landing area, steps lead onto the top of the cliffs, formed from amazingly curved lava columns. The cliff scenery and views to Mull and the mainland are superb. Seabirds are not so numerous as on Lunga but still plentiful, and include puffins and eider ducks, which breed here. The walking is easy along the grassy cliff tops, the only problem is the time restriction. Most trips only give you an hour on Staffa and 1.5 – 2 hours on Lunga.

26 AROS PARK (OS Sheet 47)

About a mile south of Tobermory on the A848 Craignure road, a signed forestry road leads to the car park and picnic area in Aros Park, the site of a former mansion. The Forestry Commission have laid out several short, easy to follow walks through delightful grounds and woods of cypress, pine and rhododendrons.

A small lochan is fringed with water lilies. At its northern end, a fine waterfall after rain, cascades over the cliffs surrounding the grounds. There is an even more impressive second set of falls. The forest trail leads towards the shore and a bridge from which the 30 foot fall can be seen plunging through a woody dell. A broader upper falls drops some 40 feet, from the top of which is a fine view across Tobermory Bay to Ardnamurchan.

27 RUBHA NAN GALL LIGHTHOUSE (OS Sheet 47)

This offers an easy 2 mile highly scenic stroll from Tobermory. From the car park beside the shore at the south end of Tobermory, walk along the harbour past the gaily painted houses and craft shops.

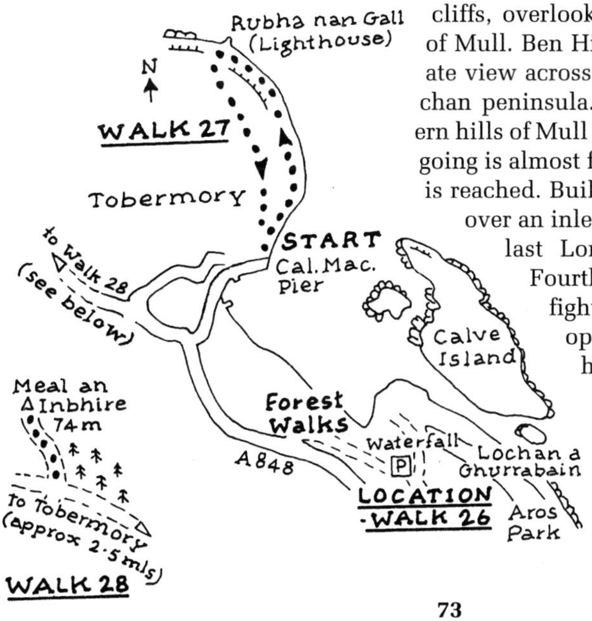

A well made path to the lighthouse, passes the Victorian built Western Isles Hotel, 50 feet above the Cal.Mac pier, then undulates gently northward through woods for 0.75 mile. It emerges onto a wide terrace between the colourful flower strewn cliffs, overlooking the picturesque Sound of Mull. Ben Hiant dominates the immediate view across the loch on the Ardnamurchan peninsula. Loch Sunart and the eastern hills of Mull are also well displayed. The going is almost flat now until the lighthouse is reached. Built in 1857, it stands sentinel over an inlet known as Bloody Bay. The last Lord of the Isles, John the Fourth, lost a great sea battle here, fighting his son Angus Og who opposed his weakness. John having conceded much of the family power by allowing King James III to deprive him of the Earldom of Ross. If you follow the path round the coast for a short distance beyond the lighthouse, some fine cliff scenery is your reward.

The gentlest return is by your outward route. However, if you don't mind a short ascent, a path just to the south of the lighthouse climbs easily to the top of the cliffs, leading in a short distance to Tobermory golf course. Taking care not to interfere with the greens or players, follow the edge of the course back into town, enjoying the enchanting view out across Calve Island and Tobermory Bay.

This short walk can be combined with the small Mull Museum in Main Street, Tobermory (open Mon – Sat) and the tiny Tobermory distillery which offers tours (Easter – Sept. Mon – Fri)

28 MEALL AN INBHIRE (OS Sheet 47)

Climbing WNW out of Tobermory, a narrow road climbs up over low hills towards Glengorm Castle. Just beyond the point where the road emerges from forest, some 2.5 miles from Tobermory, a broad rough track leads up to the radio masts on Meall an Inbhire (grid ref. 456566). This short, gentle climb brings a dramatic view of the northern part of Mull and the Ardnamurchan Peninsula.

Distance 1 mile, Height Gain 242 ft/ 74m

29 THE FOSSIL TREES OF MULL (OS Sheet 47)

Under the auspices of the National Trust for Scotland, MacCulloch's Tree on the Burg Estate, is a fossil cast of a coniferous tree some 40 feet high and 50 million years old. It is only accessible at low tide, to strong walkers, taking the path from Tiroran on the north shore of Loch Scridain 1.5 miles SW of the B8035. It involves 14 miles and a steep descent to the shore via an iron ladder. It is impossible for dogs to negotiate this.

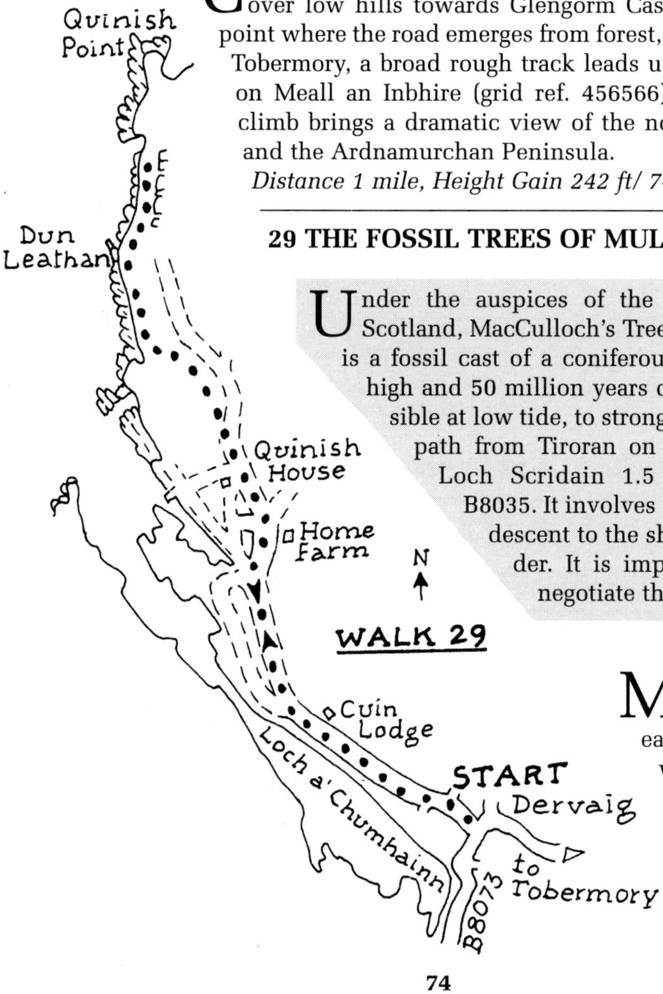

Much less well known but much easier to visit, are the well preserved lava casts of fossil trees on the shoreline near Dun Leatham, north of Dervaig. Dervaig is a small, pretty village with quaint cottages, an unusual pencil shaped church spire dating from 1905 and probably the smallest professional theatre in the world.

Leave the village by a minor road heading NW to Cuin Lodge, just above the sea inlet of Loch a' Chumhainn. From the road end, follow the track northward, forking right at each junction and passing Home Farm and Quinish House. Pass the first gate beyond Quinish House and in 250 yards bear left. Ahead of you a wall crosses the track. Keeping this on the left, head seaward towards the ruins of old Dervaig village. To reach the trees, continue along the shore for a further half a mile. They lie below the high water line under some crags. The trunk and root system of the largest tree are still discernible. One can continue along the shore to Quinish Point enjoying views to Ardnamurchan, Coll and Tiree.

Distance 5.5 miles (gentle throughout)

Whilst in the area, you may wish to visit the **Old Byre Heritage Centre**, 1 mile south of Dervaig (open daily Easter – Oct), which includes an interesting video on Mull's history.

30 EAS FORS WATERFALL & ISLE OF ULVA (OS Sheet 47)

Ulva offers a quiet retreat and a variety of walks with excellent views to various parts of Mull and outlying islands. En route to the short ferry crossing, take time to explore one of the most spectacular coastal waterfalls in Scotland. It lies beside the B8073 road on Loch Tuath, 2 miles north of Ulva. Much of the falls are below the road and easily missed. The Allt an Eas Fors thunders some 100 feet into a deep sea pool which is covered at high tide. At low tide it is possible to take a path down to the shore, a short distance from the fall. Right above the lowest fall is another 20 foot cascade. Above the road, lie another 5 falls, all worth exploring. Ulva has a distinctive shape thanks to the volcanic lavas which have been laid down in terraces edged with columnar basalt. As with much of western Scotland, the island is littered with the ruins of deserted homes, poignant reminders of the Highland Clearances which decimated the population. In the early 19th century, the island had prospered as an important supplier of kelp which was burnt and its ash used in the making of soap and glass. Following the Napoleonic Wars, the importation of cheaper substitutes, signalled the death knell of the industry. In the 4 years following the 1847 potato famine, 73 families were evicted. Today just a handful of people eke out a living here. Near the ferry is a tearoom and visitor centre which expounds on the history of the island.

Five waymarked trails have been laid out by the island's owner. A short one hour trail keeps to the roads around a farm and the church designed by Thomas Telford. Also easy is the woodland walk close to the shore. The 3 hours Livingstone Trail is for those with an historical bent. It includes the ruins of the parental home of missionary David Livingstone and a cave where evidence of Mesolithic habitation has been found. Another 3 hour walk with good views to Ben More and southern Mull, explores the south side of Ulva. The path weaves around the lava terraces westwards towards an island studded bay. It passes near the ruins of Ormaig mill, its millstones still intact, situated on a terrace above the dramatic basaltic columns at Caisteal. The Gometra Trail is a full day hike across the length of the island, following the undulating rough road above the rocky northern shore. To the western edge of Gometra and return is 17 miles. For more details of each of the trails, leaflets are available on Ulva and at Mull's tourist offices.

Note *Ulva ferry runs on demand Mon – Sat April, May & Sept, and daily June - August*
There is no accommodation on Ulva though wild camping may be possible with permission. Tel 01688 500226

31 ENVIRONS OF LOCHBUIE (OS Sheets 48 & 49)

A minor road to the hamlet of Lochbui, turns off the A849 in Glen More, at Strathcoil. The route passes lovely Loch Uisg. Surrounded by low, craggy hills and natural woodland, it is reminiscent of the Trossachs in the southern Highlands. There is parking in Lochbuie just beyond the wonderful tiny post office made of plywood. It looks as though it has been thrown together from drift-wood. The hamlet lies in a picturesque setting, overlooked to the north by rugged Ben Buie and Beinn nan Gobhar whilst to the south are the lower hills of the Laggan Forest. North of Lochbuie House, is the only circle of standing stones in Mull. The 8 stones around 6 feet high, date from the 2nd century. The circle can be approached from the bridge near the few surviving crofts.

Along the shore for several miles, on a virtually flat track, the gentle walk west-wards, is delightful. Soon after the start, a high cliff is passed, pockmarked with large caves used as sheep shelters and fishermens' net stores. The small sandy beach beyond, at port a' Bheoil Mhoir, stands in an enchanting setting in sight of Moy Castle, overlooked by craggy Creach Beinn. Natural woodland often lines the track or edges the cliffs. On the next beach, are two smooth rocks, sculptured by the sea into Henry Moore shapes. One has three paps, just like the Paps of Jura, vis-ible from here on a clear day. Strong walkers may wish to continue westward along the path for a further 3 miles to Carsaig's imposing cliffs, passing further intrigu-ing settings. Most walkers however, will be content to turn back at this point and save a little energy for the stroll to Moy Castle. On your return to Lochbuie, it is a gentle 0.75 mile stroll along a track to the well preserved 15th century 3 storey tower with a dungeon and a well in the floor of the kitchen, which refills to a set level as fast as it is emptied. The tower has stood empty since it was vacated by the MacLeans in 1752. Whenever a member of the House of Lochbuie is dying, a head-less ghost is said to ride furiously around the tower. You can walk right upto the tower although entry is forbidden, owing to the dangerous state of the upper masonry.

Another gentle and scenic walk lies closeby. East of Lochbuie, take a minor road along the south shore of Loch Spelve. From the road end at Craggan, an easy track swings round the coast to the unspoilt beach at Porterfield approximately 2 miles away, with fine views over the Firth of Lorn.

32 ASCENT OF STOB COIRE A' CHEARCAILL 770m / 2527ft

'The peak of the circular corrie' is the highest point in NE Ardgour. Lying close to the confluence of Loch Eil and Loch Linnhe, it affords grandiose 360 degree panoramic vistas. Unlike the other Corbetts in the area, its ascent is straightforward both in summer conditions and under snow, and it is reasonably situated for walkers without cars staying in the Fort William area.

The most attractive route begins at Stronchreggan on Loch Linnhe, 8.4 miles north east of the Corran Ferry. Take the track from the road bridge following the north bank of the Allt Sron a' Chreagain through the picturesque glen. Cataracts lie along the course of the wide river, fringed with gorse, birch and holly. The Corbett extends two steep sided ridges enclosing the valley, culminating in the summit at its head, perched above sizeable broken crags. To the east, the deeply gashed western flanks of Ben Nevis soar above Loch Linnhe.

About 1.25 miles along the valley, approximately 200 yards before the last fence, aim for a gate a little above the track. Beyond the fence one can make a very steep rising traverse NW onto the ridge of Braigh Bhlaich which can be followed to the summit. Longer but more preferable is to follow the fence to the right for about quarter of a mile then dog-leg back left ascending moderately steep grass and heather slopes which form the eastern end of the long ridge. The crest of the ridge itself is very gentle. Initially the slopes are broad with boggy depressions to work around but within a mile become much drier, stonier and better defined; a stately highway above Loch Eil. The hill is rich in deer and moorland birds with vibrant frogs seemingly inhabiting every tiny marshy pool.

A huge cairn and an adjacent trig point mark the airy summit above precipitous Coire a' Chearcaill. Countless rugged peaks are finely arrayed to the north and west beyond Loch Eil, whilst southward, wild Ardgour and the more rounded hills of Morvern draw the eye to the eastern end of Mull and part of Loch Linnhe. Fort William and Corpach are dwarfed by mighty Ben Nevis and Aonach Mor. Glen Spean, Beinn a' Bheithir and the peaks of Glen Coe are also well seen.

It is easiest to return the same way although it would be feasible to return to Stronchreggan via the more complicated ridge swinging SE then eastward above Gleann Sron a' Chreagain.

FACT FILE
Distance: 9 miles Height gain 770m / 2527ft
Time: 5.5 – 6.5 hours
Start/Finish: Stronchreggan Loch Linnhe GR 070725 OS Sheet 41
Remarks: Limited roadside parking at start, please ensure farm/field access is not blocked.
Stalking: Cona Glen estate restrict access 15 August - 20 October, tel. the stalker 01855 841304 or West Highland Estates 01397 702433
Public Transport: Fort William – Camasnagual passenger ferry 2 miles from start.

EASY ALTERNATIVE
The attractive first mile of the above walk is easy and on a reasonable track. For other picturesque, and peaceful, though longer valley walks, go to Inverscaddle Bay 4.5 miles to the south. On the south bank of the River Scaddle a path signed for 'Strontian' gains access to Glen Scaddle. On the north side of the River Scaddle, access can be gained to the adjacent Cona Glen through which a good track stretches for many miles.

33 ASCENT OF SGURR NA H-EANCHAINNE 730m / 2396ft

'The peak of the brains' is a relatively unfrequented, craggy, pointed peak dominating the hamlet of Corran on the western shore of Loch Linnhe. Although not the highest hill in the region, it affords absorbing, far reaching views along the loch and eastward to dramatic Glencoe. The short ascent is only recommended in clear conditions, not only for the vistas but to avoid potential route finding difficulties.

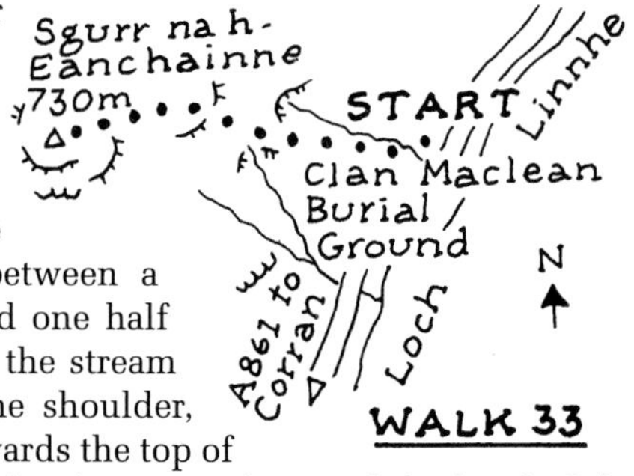

Head northward from Corran for approximately 1.7 miles along the A861 to a cattle grid beyond the Clan Maclean burial ground where the stock grazing fencing ends and allows access to the hillside. Sgurr na h-Eanchainne extends a very steep grassy shoulder between a nameless burn close to the cattle grid and one half mile to the south. Take the north bank of the stream for a short way, cross over and climb the shoulder, weaving between small rock outcrops. Towards the top of the shoulder, where it begins to level out, head westward around the head of the next stream which in its lower course cuts a significant gorge. Beyond this stream head steeply towards the sharp summit, keeping to grassy corridors between the rock outcrops. The most scenic descent retraces your outward route.

FACT FILE
Distance: 2.5 miles Height gain: 730m / 2396ft
Time: 3.5 – 4 hours

Start/Finish: A861 north of Corran GR 015657 OS Sheets 40 & 41
Remarks: Tricky in hillfog and under winter conditions
Stalking: Cona Glen estate restrict access 15 August – 20 October. Tel (stalker) 01855 841304 or West Highland Estates 01397 702433
Public Transport: buses from Fort William to Oban, Glasgow & Kinlochleven pass the Corran Ferry

EASY OPTION
Some 3 miles westward from Corran, the A861 road crosses the wide River Gour at the entrance to Glen Gour, a valley flanked by impressive high cliff-girt mountains. About quarter of a mile south of the bridge, a narrow road gives access to a path running through the glen on the south side of the river passing Loch nan Gabhar. The walking is very gentle though there are rough and boggy patches. Distance optional, one can continue all the way to Strontian, some 16 miles away.

34 ASCENT OF GARBH BHEINN (ARDGOUR) 885m / 2905ft

This is a complex Corbett that walkers, and climbers, wax lyrical over. Not named *'rough hill'* for nothing, its jagged skyline draws the discerning eye when viewed from the east across Loch Linnhe at Ballachulish. Try and save this outing for a fine day for the superb views and spectacular rock extravaganza that the mountain itself displays.

There are two recommended routes which both begin at a large parking area on the A861, near the bridges over the river issuing from Coire an Iubhair (kora an yoo-ir), 1000 yards west of the buildings of Inversanda Estate. For less experienced walkers, the easiest line of ascent crosses the road bridge and bears NW up the long but moderate ridge of Sron a' Garbh Choire Bhig. The going is essentially grassy, weaving a way between innumerable small crags and boulders with traces of path. From the cairn, take time to savour the vistas of the Morvern hills and east across Loch Linnhe to Glencoe and the Creran hills, whilst nearer at hand, the dramatic rocky amphitheatre surrounding Coire an Iubhair culminates in the huge cliff girt south face of Garbh Bheinn. The col beyond, (748m) is reached by a moderate, broad rocky ridge. A straightforward but steeper, rockier climb, gains the short west ridge of Garbh Bheinn (garven). The summit is airily situated on the brink of the southern cliffs.

To complete a circular walk, retrace your steps to the 748m col then head NE dropping steeply into the corrie below, aiming for the south bank of a small stream. A poor path on grass wends down between the crags and boulders. Cross the Abhainn Coire an Iubhair to pick up a clear though often very boggy path on the north bank, which follows the river back down to the car park.

A superb, though more strenuous traverse encircles the whole of Coire an Iubhair. It is recommended only for those walkers with scrambling and route finding experience and in good conditions. Using the same start, the route heads NE up on to the broad grassy ridge of Druim an Iubhair. Initially steep, the going eases though remains somewhat rough and hummocky. Continuing onto Sgor Mhic

Eacharna above lonely Glen Gour, the ridge becomes increasingly rocky and scree covered as it drops steeply down, then climbs again over Beinn Bheag. The last half mile to its west top is much easier. Across the head of Coire an Iubhair, a plethora of crags, towers and buttresses plunge to the corrie. The north east buttress of Garbh Bheinn is particularly awesome.

Beinn Bheag drops steeply away in a series of slabs towards Coire an Iubhair but an easy if steep gully avoids any difficulties in the descent towards the Bealach Feith 'n Amean at the head of the corrie. A faint path and the remains of an old fence lead to the col's tiny lochan, lying in a dramatic setting beneath the thousand foot northern crags of Garbh Bheinn. From the lochan, a steep, grassy gully offers the easiest ascent of the face, above which, some easy scrambling is required to reach the summit, along the left hand rim of the NW corrie. *(Avoid straying to the east of the face, where the rocks are at their steepest and scrambling is more difficult).* Descent can then be made by either of the aforementioned easier routes.

All the above routes can be confusing in mist and if foul weather hits whilst you are on the summit, there is a quick escape route. From the 748m col east of the summit, head south down into Coire a' Chrothrium, to reach the A861 in Glen Tarbert 2.25 miles from the start point. This is actually the most direct and quickest way to ascend the mountain but is not normally recommended, being steep heather, scree and gravel which drops over 2500 feet in just over a mile.

FACT FILE
Distance: 6 miles Height gain: 3050 ft/ 930m (longer traverse 7.5 miles 4300 ft / 1280m)
Time: 5 – 6 hours (7 – 8 hours)
Start / Finish: A861 near Inversanda GR 929597 OS Sheet 40 (starts on sheet 49)
Remarks: In hillfog or under winter conditions, this complex craggy mountain is inadvisable to inexperienced walkers
Stalking season: during Sept., Oct., & Jan. enquire at Inversanda House Tel. 01855 841305 or 841275
Public Transport: Corran ferry daily. Weekday bus service from Ardgour to Kilchoan, passes through Inversanda

EASY OPTION
Although inclined to be boggy, the easy path leading into Coire an Iubhair is well worth following, being a wild and dramatic glacial valley. The imposing craggy buttresses and ridges of Garbh Bheinn gradually hove into view, culminating after three miles in the awesome north east face.

35 KINGAIRLOCH TO GLENSANDA

This coastal walk enables one to explore the delightfully situated hamlet of Kingairloch and part of the roadless sections of the Morvern shoreline alongside Loch Linnhe with views across the water to Lismore Island and the hills of Appin and North Lorn. There is little climbing involved although the path can occasionally be rather wet and slightly rough underfoot. After heavy rain, some burn crossings may require a short, shallow paddle.

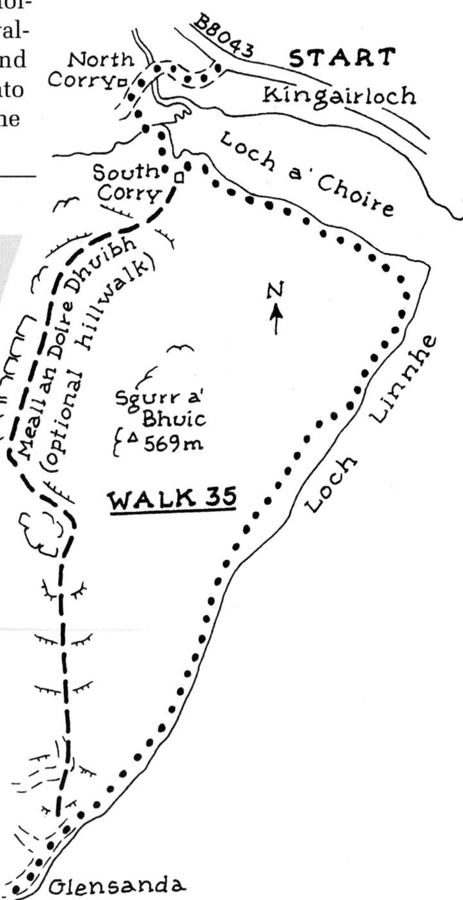

The public are not allowed to drive down the private road into Kin-gairloch from the B8043. Just over a mile up the B road to the north west of this road junction, an obvious track turns off to the left, descending through a short tract of forest. On reaching the private road turn right and follow it past the scattering of houses grandly set beneath a ring of high, rugged hills. The road and river are fringed with wonderful old moss carpeted trees and an abundance of rhododendrons. Semi- tame deer are often seen hereabout. Three stags posed perfectly for me and did not twitch a muscle although I was within 20 yards of them. Unfortunately it was raining and I hadn't bothered with a camera.

About 50 yards before the large white house of North Corry, veer off the road onto the grass to your left and follow the fence, passing through a small gate. Just beyond is a junction of 3 ways. Ignoring the main track, head slightly left through a gateway into a large field. Aim for the small coniferous coppice on the far side of the field, to the right of a line of telegraph poles. Go through a gate and over a bridge into the trees. On the far side, cross over 2 more bridges and take the path leading towards the grey house of South Corry. Beside the house the path isn't obvious. Head for the left corner of a small plantation of trees just above the shore and you'll soon pick up the path once more. This leads above the shoreline of Loch a' Choire to gain Loch Linnhe. The path continues above the loch for a further 4.5 miles to Glensanda where lie the remains of a partly restored 15th century castle. Unfortunately this is now dwarfed by the huge Glensanda stone quarry. On weekdays one probably won't want to get too close because of the intrusive noise.

Most walkers will have to retrace their steps although hillwalkers have the option of ascending the path climbing steeply behind South Corry House up Meall an Doire Dhuibh before descending to Glensanda and returning via the coastal path.

FACT FILE

Distance optional, to Glensanda and return: 13 miles
Time: 6 hours
(Kingairloch to Ardtornish: 15.5 miles 8 hours)
Start/Finish: B8043 road GR 841532 OS Sheet 49
Stalking season: check locally first if considering the route over Meall an Doire Dhuibh. Check with Ardtornish Estate if continuing onto their ground (tel: 01967 421288, 20 Aug-21 Sept).

36 THE BLACK GLEN

Morvern is blessed with a number of beautiful stretches of native woodland which are home to a rich variety of mammals, birdlife and flora. One of the most accessible woods lies in Gleann Dubh, the "black glen" which runs north of Acharn. A track running through the attractive glen offers gentle, sheltered walking. The first 2.5 miles to Crosben are particularly rewarding. Don't forget the binoculars!

About 4 miles north of Lochaline, Acharn Farm lies close to the main road on the west side of the Black Water river. (There is parking on the east side of the river but ensure farm access is not blocked). An obvious track leads gently northward above the east side of the river through Glean Dubh, the eastern fringe of the Scottish Wildlife Trust's Rahoy Hills Reserve. The first 100 yards are rather muddy but thereafter the going is generally good underfoot. The route passes through oakwood for the first mile, below the moorland hills which drop abruptly to a narrow, sheer sided gorge with the lively river often out of sight. The valley begins to open out in a further half mile. For those wanting a long walk and not wishing to retrace their steps, the path continues up the quiet and unspoilt valley until it reaches the road some 7 rniles north of Acharn. On Fridays only during the school term, a bus travels south along this road towards Lochaline (at present about Spm) which would save a long road walk. For hillwalkers, an alternative to the road, (provided the water level of the Black Water is not too high), would be to return over Beinn Chlaonleud, a long and very rough, pathless hill which forms the eastern flank of Gleann Dubh. *(Should you wish to return through the hills to the west of the glen, it is essential to contact the Ardtornish Estate Office or the Scottish Wildlife Trust warden first. The habitats the Trust are trying to preserve, are extremely fragile).*

Start/ Finish: Acharn 703505

Distance Optional

Remarks: For more information on the Scottish Wildlife Trust's Rahoy Hills Reserve, enquire at the Ardtornish Estate office by Ardtornish House. Stalking season: Usually no restrictions but check with Ardtornish Estate 20 Aug. - 21 Sept tel. 01967 421288. If walking beyond Crosben, also contact Laudale Estate (West Highland Estate Office) 01397 702433

37 WALKS FROM KINLOCH

Walkers of all abilities will find something to suit around peaceful and picturesque Loch Teacuis on the western fringe of Morvern. To the south, coniferous forest rises towards an escarpment with striking narrow bands of volcanic rocks strung across the hillside like a layered cake. Deciduous woodland along the north shore fronts rounded crag topped hills looking out to Ben Hiant on the Ardnamurchan Peninsula. Wildlife enthusiasts should bring binoculars, the area being rich in a variety of birds and mammals. The loch is one of the finest places to spot wild otters in the country. One couple has been visiting here for about 20 years, specifically to watch these delightful creatures. Stealth and patience will, however, be required.

The road ends half a mile south of the farm at Kinloch. Unfortunately, the estate does not cater for tourist parking. Go early, there is sufficient space for only 2 cars on the roadside verge. Latecomers may need to park as much as a mile away. From the road end, a track bears off to the left and follows above the south shore through the coniferous plantations which rather limit views. More pleasurable is to continue straight ahead on the rough road swinging round the head of the shallow bay and undulating along the north shore. The track ends at Rahoy after 2 miles but it is possible to continue beside the rocky shore.

For those preferring a scenic hillwalk, follow the north shore track as far as the holiday home of Caorann about a mile beyond Kinloch. Behind the house a peat and grass track rises over the flowery moorland above the loch, to reach a grassy bowl under **Beinn Ghormaig 452m / 1483ft;** its summit dome fringed by small bands of crags. Within the bowl it is easy to lose the path as there is a confusing number of animal and vehicular tracks. Aim across the tussocky grass to the Bealach Sloc an Eich, the pass to the immediate left of Beinn Ghormaig. Once into the pass, the narrow path becomes clear and traverses the lower slopes of the hill to reach a cairn and a delectable view of much of Loch Sunart and the entire Ardnamurchan Peninsula with the Inner Hebrides beyond. The estate requests that you return by your outward route to avoid unnecessary disturbance to wildlife or estate activities.

FACT FILE

Distance: To Bealach cairn and return 6.5 miles, height gain 330m/ 1083ft
Time: 3 -- 3.5 hours
Start/Finish: Kinloch road end GR656542

38 ARDTORNISH CASTLE & THE SOUND OF MULL

About 2.5 miles north of Lochaline, a narrow road tums off the A884 towards the imposing towers of Ardtornish, a Victorian mansion set in 28 acres of attractive grounds, surrounded by rolling moorland hills at the head of Loch Aline.

Just before the car park and gardens (open to the public), a rough, virtually flat road bears off to the right and follows the eastern shore of the loch southward, passing below stands of deciduous woodland and later, grazing land and open moorland. This provides very gentle and scenic walking. Loch Aline translates as 'beautiful loch'. In 3.25 miles you reach Old Ardtornish Steading. *(Note that this point can easily be reached by bicycle).* If you leave the track and continue southward above the sea, you soon come to the ruins of Ardtornish Castle, standing on a small headland overlooking the picturesque Sound of Mull. Built in 1340, it remained an important stronghold for the Lords of the Isles until the late 15th century. They controlled a huge region extending from Loch Nevis to South Argyll in addition to the Western Isles. Following the defeat of the Jacobites, this whole area was laid waste in 1746 by the Hanovarian troops.

For those wishing to extend the walk, the gentle going continues eastward for another 2.5 miles to Innir~nore. Return to the Steading and carry on down the hill to a hairpin bend. Leave the road and head eastward towards a large and obvious

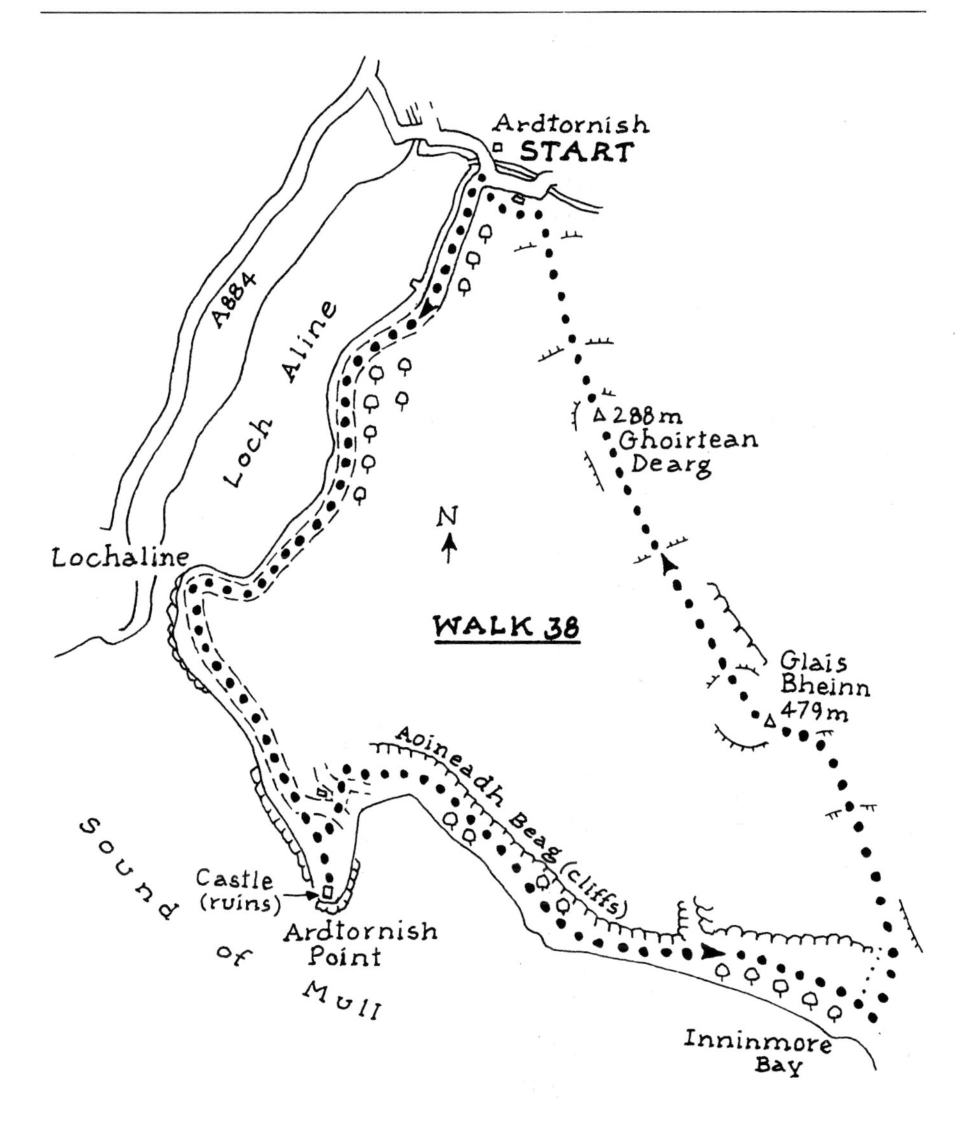

pine tree about 500 yards away. A distinct path now leads through pretty woodland above the Sound of Mull under the high cliffs of Aoineadh Beag. This protected woodland is a Site of Special Scientific Interest with a rich variety of mosses, liverworts and other flora. Numerous strearns are crossed which are impressive after heavy rain, though can become rather slippery.

Rather than retrace your steps, you can climb the steep slopes above ~ninrnore and return to the Steading along the top of the cliffs. For hillwalkers, another alternative from the top of the cliffs above Inninmore, is to continue northward over gradual but rough moorland onto Glais Bheinn 479m/ 1572ft, an excellent viewpoint for eastern Mull and southern Morvern. From the trig point, long, gentle moorland slopes lead NNW back to Ardtornish.

FACT FILE

Distance optional: to Ardtornish Castle return 7.5 miles, time 2.5 – 3 hours
To Inninmore return 12.5 miles (7 miles can be cycled) 5 – 6 hours
Inninmore & Glais Bheinn 10.5 miles, 500m / 1640ft of ascent, 6 hours
Start/Finish: Ardtornish GR 703474 OS Sheet 49
Remarks: Bicycles can be hired from Ardtornish Estate Office Visitor Centre. Pamphlets also on sale re the local flora & fauna. Staff are happy to recommend other walks within the estate.
Stalking season: Usually no restrictions but do check with the estate office 20 Aug – 21 Sept (tel. 01967 421288)

39 DRIMNIN TO AULISTON

The scenic B849 road running north-westwards from Lochaline along the Sound of Mull ends at the hamlet of Drimnin. Some 2.5 miles to the north lie the ruined houses of Auliston, reached by a gentle climb. One hundred tenants were evicted from here in 1855 to the nearby Isle of Oronsay on Loch Sunart, only to be removed once more in 1868. In contrast to the sad ruins, panoramic vistas towards Mull and Ardnamurchan are delightful.

Entering Drimnin, the road descends to a bridge over the Abhainn Mhungasdail. There is parking a short way beyond. Walk back towards the bridge and take the private road branching off to the left signed 'Drimnin Estate' and 'Mains Cottage 1.5 miles'. The rough road climbs easily northward through delightful, deciduous woodland. After 1000 yards, bear right over a stile onto a track signed 'An Doirlinn 5 miles'. The next 400 yards of mud track have been badly churned up by cattle. On reaching a track junction, keep

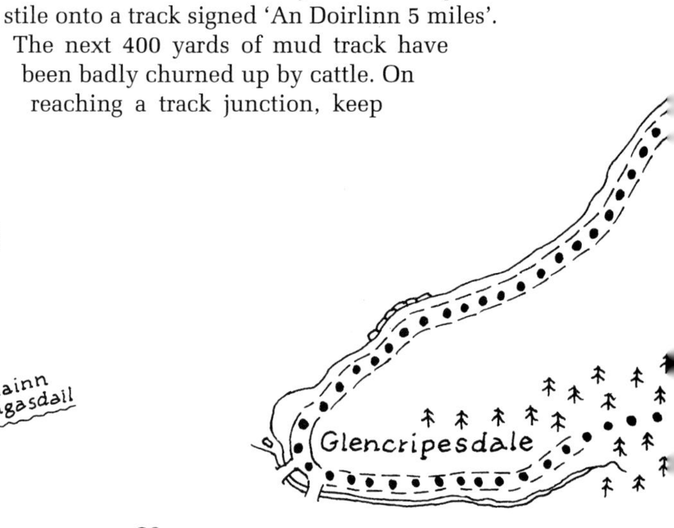

straight on uphill. Immediately the going underfoot improves dramatically. Well scattered trees and a huge blaze of gorse provide a wonderful foreground to the increasingly enchanting prospect across the sound to the mountains of Mull. Open moorland is soon reached extending the vistas to Ardnamurchan dominated by Ben Hiant, with part of the Inner and Outer Hebrides eventually peeping through. After 2 miles, a ruined croft is seen slightly below to your left. A gate to the left of the track gives access to the sheep grazings high above the sea. Head NNW (aim for Ben Hiant) across the grass for 0.5 mile losing just a little height to gain the ruins of Auliston.

Having returned to the track, you can climb for another 0.25 mile to a high point. Unfortunately owing to recent forestry plantings, views beyond here are severely restricted to seaward. Given the roughness of the terrain hereabouts, it is advisable to return via your outward route.

FACT FILE
Distance: 5 miles. Height gain 170m/ 558ft
Time: 2 - 3 hours

40 GEARR CHREAG AND LOCH SUNART

The north side of Loch Sunart is enchantingly wooded but this restricts views greatly. The south shore is more open though much is roadless and one needs to walk to fully appreciate its beauty. Wonderfully panoramic walks are available, catering for all abilities.

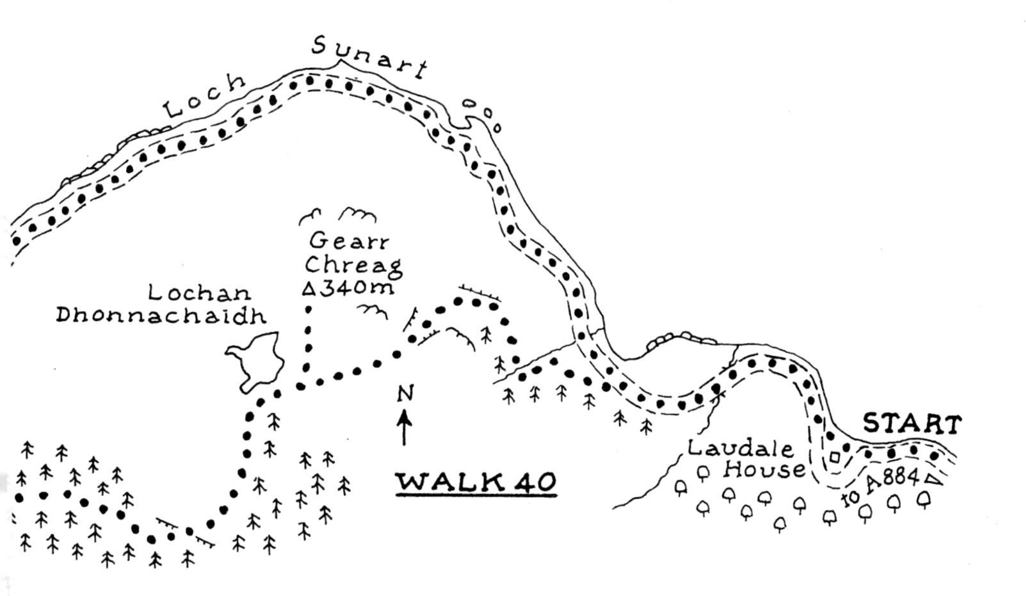

Just as the A884 road turns away from the loch towards Lochaline, a minor road bears right and winds above the shore for nearly 2 miles to within half a mile of Laudale House. Limited parking slots can be found approaching the road end. There is a huge turning circle but bear in mind when parking that heavy timber lorries may wish to turn here.

For those just desiring an easy stroll, a good track leads gently westwards, passing Laudale. This is a grand spot. The large white house is backed by oakwood and rough, steep sided hills. Across the loch, craggy Beinn Resipol dominates with Garbh Bheinn rising imposingly to the east, the finest mountain in the region. Otters frequent the loch and seals are often seen close to shore. With forest and moorland reaching down to the sea, there is a great variety of birdlife. Apart from a brief climb away from the loch, the main track undulates above Loch Sunart all the way to Glencripsdale. It is particularly entrancing on a fine summer's evening.

For hillwalkers, **Gearr Chreag** rising some 3 miles to the west of Laudale offers a breathtaking prospect inspite of its modest height (340m/ 1116ft). About a mile west of Laudale House, take the second track on the left beyond the river ford. This climbs steadily through thick forest with the occasional fine view to Loch Sunart. Above the tree line, a distinct grassy path (mainly good underfoot) continues to climb gently. Extensive vistas now open up over the loch and eastward along Glen Tarbert to the distinctive Pap of Glencoe. Within a mile, a narrow pass is reached just above Lochan Dhonnachaidh looking out to Ben Hiant on the Ardnamurchan Peninsula. From the pass head due north for 700 yards over rough pathless moorland interspersed with small slabby knolls. The panoramas from hills with triangulation pillars are usually excellent and Gearr Chreag is no exception. Virtually the whole of Loch Sunart is on show surrounded by wild and spectacular craggy hills. North of Salen harbour, part of Lochs Shiel and Moidart are visible. All the major hills of Skye can be easily discerned. Eigg and the Rum Cuillin show equally well and on a clear day one can see to the southern Outer Hebrides.

You can retrace your steps to complete an easy half day outing. For those preferring a long day's hike, return to the narrow pass then continue along the path descending south then westward into the forest of Glen Cripsdale. There is a National Nature Reserve around Glencripsdale, the deciduous woodland being home to some 200 varieties of flowering plants and ferns. The reserve is fenced off to the public but many plants can be seen around the path itself. A track is joined above the wide river and continues to a tiny bay on Loch Sunart. The track above the shore is then followed back to Laudale.

FACT FILE

Distance: Gearr Chreag return 8.5 miles Height gain: 340m / 1116ft (Glencripsdale circular 17 miles with height gain 420m/ 1378ft)
Time: 4 – 4.5 hours (8 hours)
Start/Finish: Laudale Loch Sunart, GR 756598 OS Maps 49 & 40
Remarks: do not tackle the extension to Glencripsdale unless you are confident of your fitness. The area is remote with help a long way off.
Stalking season: Laudale Estate, see local notices. Check locally for restrictions.

41 THE ASCENT OF BEINN RESIPOL 2774ft / 845m

Rising majestically in splendid, rugged isolation between Lochs Sunart and Shiel, this shapely Corbett should be on all hillwalkers tick-lists. Try and save for a clear day; the summit panorama being one of the most extensive and magnificent of any hill along the whole western seaboard. It will also avoid any route finding difficulties. The origin of the name Beinn Resipol (*byn reshapol*) is unclear, possibly from old Norse for a homestead given the farm at its southern foot. More likely is *'the cairn above the pool'* from an inlet to the north on Loch Shiel formed by the River Polloch, poll being Gaelic for pool.

The easiest route is from Resipol Farm, 8 miles west of Strontian along the A861 on the shores of Loch Sunart. Rather than return the same way, if you can make use of the one daily bus, a cycle or a second car, then the best expedition continues eastward from the summit before swinging down towards Ardnastang, 1 mile west of Strontian.

Just beyond the road bridge over the Allt Mhic Chiarain at Resipole, take a track on the west bank of the river. This quickly crosses to the eastern bank and narrows to a good path, climbing through deciduous woodland above a series of deep river gorges. A mile on, the path emerges onto open moorland. The path now becomes rather boggy and very intermittent but keep following the south bank of the stream eastward. Where the stream divides around the 530m mark, leave it and head onto the steep west ridge and follow it to the summit. The going is essentially grassy with small rocky outcrops. It is feasible to follow the upper right hand tributary of the stream to Lochan Bac an Lochain but this leaves an even steeper climb, weaving between a maze of crags on grassy terraces.

From the summit cone, the craggy northern flanks fall away steeply to Loch Shiel and a clutch of rugged Moidart peaks. Further afield when conditions allow, the spectacular vistas extend to Knoydart, Torridon, Mull, Skye, Arran, Jura and the Outer Hebrides, to name but a few.

Either retrace your steps, or if descending to Strontian, take the east ridge, another grassy affair with rocky protuberances. Around 550m, near the source of the Allt Camas a' Choirce, swing SE towards Meall an t-Slugain, then head east to the Bealach nan Carn (GR 798652), to pick up the old miners' track which once served the Strontium mines at Coire an t-Suidhe, a little to the north. At the pass, old cairns are reminders of an old coffin route dating from the 6th century, when St Finan built a sanctuary on Eilean Fhianain, a tiny islet on Loch Shiel. It thereafter became a sacred burial ground and hearses were laboriously carried over the hills from Ardnastang on Loch Sunart to Loch Shiel. You should find the good path down to Ardnastang, a bit less of an effort!

FACT FILE

Distance: (full traverse) 8.5 miles, Height gain 845m / 2773ft
Time: 5 – 7 hours
Start: A861 at Resipole GR 722639. Finish: Ardnastang GR 799614 OS Sheet 40

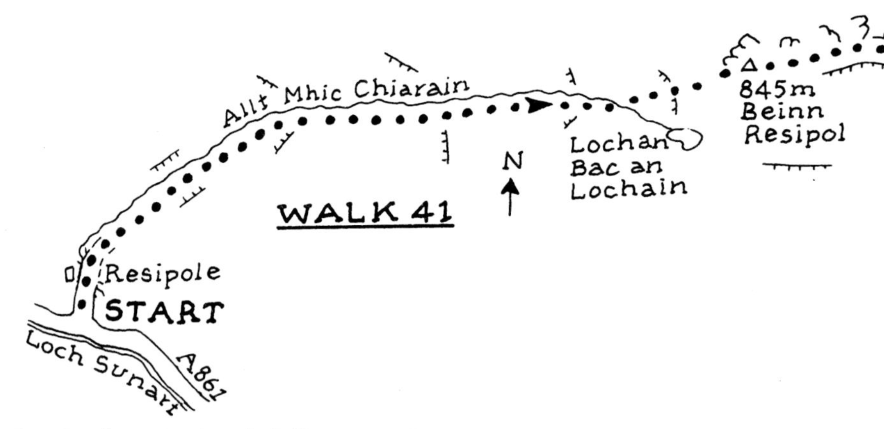

Remarks: Good navigational skills required. In hillfog it is safest to keep to west ridge route. Stray to the right too soon when descending the east ridge and you could become snarled up in very steep ground and crags
Stalking season: check local notices
Public transport: one bus runs along the A861 between Ardgour & Kilchoan daily Mon – Sat.

EASY ALTERNATIVES

41A ARIUNDLE NATURE RESERVE

One mile north of Strontian, this nature reserve in the Strontian Glen offers very gentle walking on generally well constructed paths and tracks in attractive settings. There is plenty of interest and can be enjoyed even in poor weather.

From the car park, a track leads through pretty moss covered woodland of oak, beech, rowan, hazel, spruce and larch. Although the local timber was once used by charcoal burners, it is still one of the finest examples of surviving native woodland in Scotland. Remains of the old charcoal hearths can be seen in some of the clearings further up the glen. These glades are popular with butterflies in summer. Plants thrive in the damp, mild climate including some rare lichens and liverworts. Roe deer can often be seen browsing. The trees echo to a rich variety of avian activity and the trackside ditches are alive with cavorting frogs and toads.

About half a mile up the glen, the signed 'Strontian River Walk' bears right to more open ground with good views along the valley and follows the wide river upstream; its numerous small rapids a delightful spectacle after rain. The path eventually returns into the forest to rejoin the main track. By turning left here, one can return to the car park after an enchanting walk of about 75 minutes duration. Alternatively one can turn right along the track and continue up through the afforested glen for a further 3 miles passing the aforementioned glades to reach some old lead mines.

41B AIRD ARAIGH

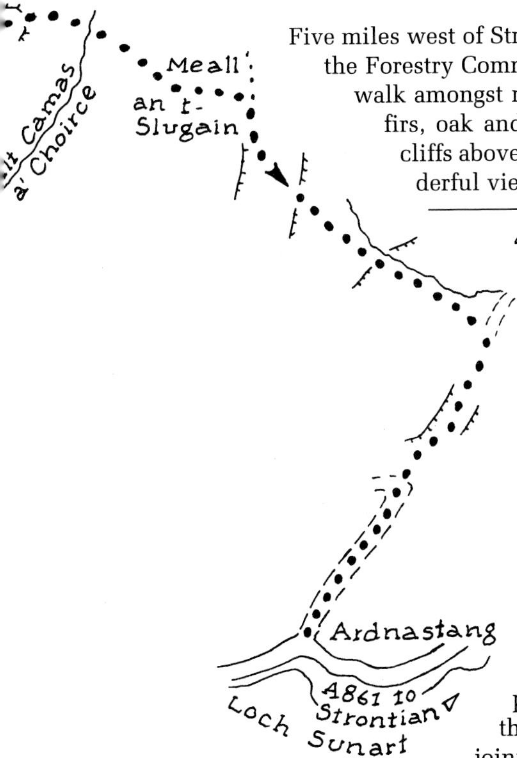

Five miles west of Strontian, from a car park beside the A861, the Forestry Commission has laid out an easy waymarked walk amongst mixed woodland including beech, silver firs, oak and Scots pine. It also encompasses some cliffs above Loch Sunart, from which there are wonderful views.

42 BOURBLAIGE - CAMAS NAN GEALL CIRCULAR

This is a short coastal walk on the Ardnamurchan Peninsula, full of scenic splendour and historic interest. All climbing is fairly gentle, although the going underfoot is slightly rough for several short stretches, and boots are an essential.

Meall an t-Slugain
Allt Camas a' Choirce
Ardnastang
A861 to Strontian
Loch Sunart

Park at the small car park above beautiful Camas nan Geall bay, 4 miles west of Glenborrodale, or in one of the three small rough laybys during the next mile of road (not the passing places). Climb the road for a mile north of the car park then turn left through a gate joining a wide track heading south westward. This skirts a small grassy bowl dominated by the steep grassy terraces of Ben Hiant. The track soon fizzles out but continue in the same direction over the rough pasture between shapely hillocks formed by volcanic cone sheets. High above the sea the ruined remains of the crofting community of Bourblaige are scattered around the large sheltered grassy hollow, above which a tall mares tail waterfall plunges. The tenants were evicted in 1828 to make way for the inevitable sheep which still graze her, sharing the pasture with small herds of deer. The views across the mouth of Loch Sunart to Morvern and north Mull are superb.

Still continuing south westward, keeping the tall knolls to your left, descend gently past the last houses and cross the burns to reach a fence a short way beyond. Turn left at the fence and follow it down easy grassy slopes to a small rocky bay dominated by the imposing cliffs of Ben Hiant's precipitious southern flanks and a hanging waterfall high above.

Turn left onto a path following the shore close to the high water mark. Over a small rise you reach a wider rocky bay, patrolled by oyster catchers and shags skimming the wave tops. Seals too can often be spied in the water. This shoreline is great for beach combers who may be lucky enough to find amethysts and cairngorms amongst the more usual marine detritus.

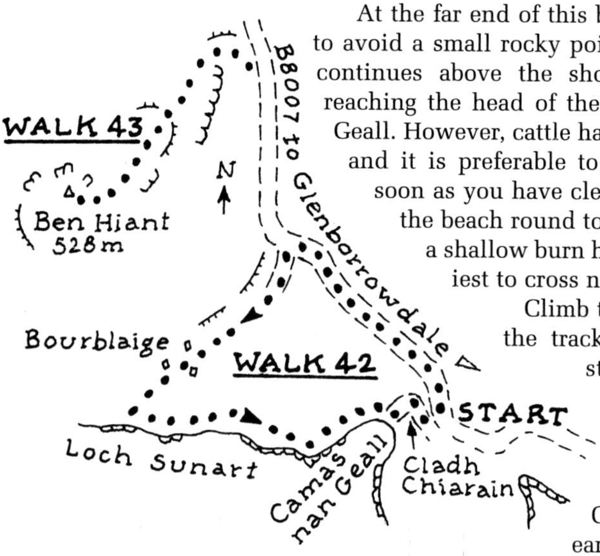

At the far end of this bay, the path climbs again to avoid a small rocky point. The correct path then continues above the shore, descending only on reaching the head of the small bay of Camas nan Geall. However, cattle have badly mashed the path and it is preferable to descend to the shore as soon as you have cleared the point and follow the beach round to the head of the bay. Here a shallow burn has to be paddled. It is easiest to cross near the sea.

Climb the enormous stile to gain the track passing the red carved stone of Cladh Chiarain which was possibly dedicated by St Columba, a monument to the 6th century Irish Saint, Ciaran. There is an even earlier standing stone with a carving of a cross and a dog thereon and the remains of an old chapel. Once over a second stile, the track can be followed back up to the car park and road.

FACT FILE

Distance: 3.5 miles Height gain 110m / 361ft

Time: 2 hours

Public Transport: Ardgour – Kilchoan bus passes start

43 ASCENT OF BEN HIANT 528m/ 1733ft

This shapely hill on the Ardnamurchan Peninsula is the highest point for many miles around and as a consequence is a superb viewpoint. On a clear day the vistas encompass Loch Sunart, much of Morvern and Mull, Coll, Rum, Skye, Eigg, Muck and even part of the Outer Hebrides. An added attraction is that unlike the vast proportion of western hills, you start way above sea level, so the climb is relatively short.

Above the bay of Camas nan Geall, the B8007 turns away from Loch Sunart and climbs up to a pass. A few yards before the head of the pass, across the road from a track, an initially narrow marshy path begins. It soon improves and climbs steeply for a short time onto the lower part of Ben Hiant's north east ridge. The gradient now eases as it follows the grassy ridge which is fringed by small, broken crags. Just below the final steeper slopes under the summit, the path divides. If the rocks are likely to be wet and greasy, then the left hand path offers the safest, although less obvious route. This traverses round to avoid steep awkward ground and gains the summit from the south. In dry conditions one can take the right hand path which climbs up quite an airy rocky slope before reaching easier grass just below the top. Owing to the precipitous nature of the hill's upper slopes, it is advisable to return the same way.

FACT FILE

Distance: 2.5 miles Height gain: 370m/ 1214ft
Time: 2.5 – 3 hours
Start/ Finish: B8007 OS Sheet 47 GR551641
Public Transport: Ardgour – Kilchoan bus passes the start

44 SANNA BAY

The scattered white painted houses of Sanna stand in an enchanting setting backed by small craggy moorland hills leading down to sheep grazing on the machair and grassy sand dunes. The bay itself is actually a series of delightful small, sandy coves with rocky promontories and numerous small islets and skerries. On a clear day, panoramic vistas extend to the Small Isles, Skye and the southern Outer Hebrides. Short walks radiate in three directions. Unless drought conditions prevail, boots are recommended as the ground is inclined to be wet over short stretches.

From the car park follow the track to the right, parallel with the sea, past the last cluster of houses. Cross the sheep pasture down to a bridge over a small burn and skirt round the rear of the house beyond. The moorland rises above the sea in a series of small cairned and flowery hillocks. The map indicates 2 paths rising to the largest of the cairns situated on a knoll above **Sanna Point.** In reality they are not easy to follow given the confusing number of sheep tracks hereabouts. They are also inclined to lead you straight into a bog. It is better to pick your own way, keeping to the higher ground wherever possible to avoid the marshy depressions be-tween the knolls. From the cairn above Sanna Point, there is a fine view back across Sanna Bay to the lighthouse on the protruding Point of Ardnamurchan. Eastward, an impressive rocky coast extends to the low cliffs around Glendrian Caves, which are actually merely fissures of no real interest. One can easily potter further along this coast towards Plocaig Bay where the gorges cleaving the cliffs are beloved by plants including prolific yellow roseroot. There is plenty of avian interest with the shags, terns, guillemots, fulmars, cormorants and gulls cheek by jowl with the smaller moorland birds. Seals too can often be

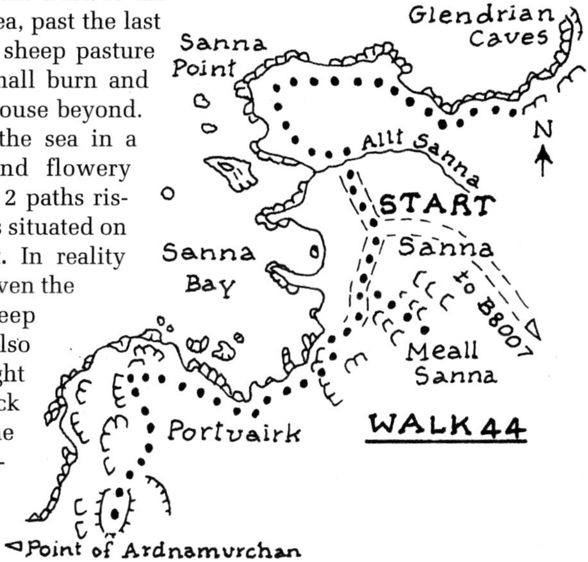

seen out to sea.
Sanna Point return 1.6 miles

Turning left at the car park, a wide track leads behind the dunes for half a mile to a low building. Thereafter a path crosses a burn then climbs a short way round the back of a small hill. From the top of the rise there is a wonderful view of Sanna Bay and to the hamlet of **Portuairk;** its white houses dotted above a rocky cove backed by moorland hills of slab and heather. Ignoring the animal tracks continuing straight ahead, the path turns down the other side of the hill and follows above the shoreline to reach the road at Portuairk. The more venturesome can take the path climbing onto the hill beyond the hamlet. You can continue south onto higher ground, working a way over the rough moorland between the slabby outcrops to reach viewpoints looking out over the Point of Ardnamurchan and southward to Mull.
Portuairk and return 2.25 miles

Hillwalkers may also like to yomp over the rough moorland between the wee slabby crags to reach the summit of Meall Sanna (GR 453685) above the houses at Sanna, a superb viewpoint in clear weather.
1 mile with 170m / 558ft height gain

45 WALKS FROM OCKLE

Most of the northern coastline of the Ardnamurchan Peninsula is roadless and the only way to explore is on foot. From the hamlet of Ockle, east of Kilmory, a long but easy track and path stretches for 7.5 miles eastward to Arivegaig in picturesque Kentra Bay on the Moidart coast. It affords lovely views seaward to the Small Isles and Skye and along the interesting rocky coast of Ardnamurchan and Moidart. There is a total absence of public transport. For a 2 car party the full traverse makes for a very enjoyable and not unduly difficult outing. Those without this luxury may prefer to sample the track from either end. For those wishing to take just one short walk, then the first 1.5 miles of track from Ockle is the most rewarding.

From the parking space at the road end at Ockle, continue uphill along the track ignoring the tracks to left and right. In 200 yards bear right beside the holiday cottage of Sruthan Ruadh. You soon pass a small, almost circular reed and lily fringed lochan where pairs of eider and mallard ducks can often be seen. Continue up the small rise passing through a gate, ignoring a track bearing off to the right. Once over the hillcrest, a fine succession of seascapes greet you as the track undu-

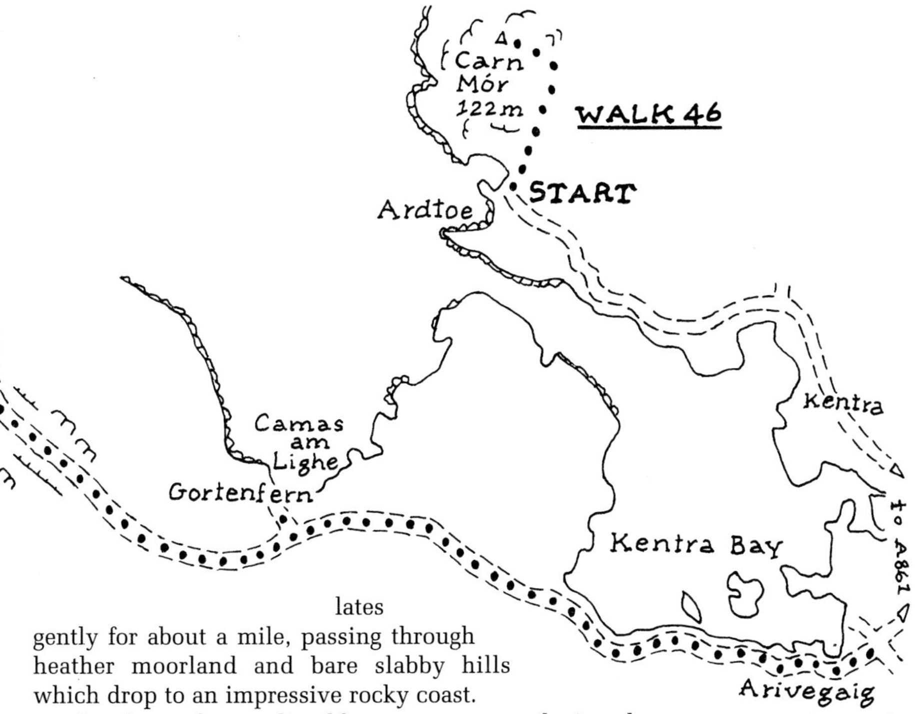

lates gently for about a mile, passing through heather moorland and bare slabby hills which drop to an impressive rocky coast.

Just beyond a tree lined burn, a narrow path signed for "Gortenfern" now heads inland, rising gently onto the moorland above a birch fringed stream. In a further 1.75 miles, the path joins a track where you turn right and follow it above the coast before gradually descending towards Gortenfern and the remote bay of Camas an Lighe. A short track to the left bears off to the bay itself where the curious sands are said to whistle or sing as you walk across them in bare feet in dry weather. The main track now undulates through forest to reach shallow Kentra Bay and the road at Arivegaig.

Distance Ockle to Arivegaig: 7.5 miles, Height gain approximately 200m/ 656ft
Time: 3 – 4 hours
Start: Ockle OS Sheet 47 GR556704. Optional Finish: Arivegaig OS Sheet 40 GR 652677.

For those preferring a short, easy walk from Ockle that visits the coast itself, then take the grassy track which bears left at the aforementioned cottage of Sruthan Ruadh and gently descends in about half a mile to a delightful secluded rocky cove with the sad ruins of an old croft looking out to the Small Isles. Some easy rock hopping around the right side of the bay brings the low lava cliffs of Ockle Point into view.

Distance: 1 mile, Height gain: 60m/ 196ft

46 ASCENT OF CARN MOR 122m/ 400ft

Considering its lack of height, this short hillwalk offers surprisingly rough, pathless going and is only suitable for sure footed walkers. It can be worth doing even when there is low hillfog inland providing it is bright to seaward. From the lowly summit above the sea there are entrancing views to the Small Isles, Skye, along Loch Moidart to Castle Tioram, Kentra Bay and a plethora of rough knobbly hills and distant Corbetts.

From the gated car park at the small, sandy cove of Ardtoe, follow the road to the end and turn right to cross a small dam. Ignoring the steps and path beyond, immediately head to the right, following the small rocky knoll down and round. Cross the dried out salt flats below a second dam to gain the base of Carn Mor. (If the flats are flooded, the friendly staff at the Marine Farming Unit at the rear of the car park will normally allow access through the maze of their buildings, to a causeway which leads to higher ground above the flats).

The summit lies to the north but it is impossible to aim directly for it. The ground is even more complicated than the map suggests with the hill comprising a number of large slabby knolls. Always keeping a little to the right of a direct line of ascent, work a way up over the rough moorland, weaving between the slabby crags. There are 2 summit cairns of similar height, several hundred yards apart. Owing to the rough nature of the ground, it is easiest to return via your outward route.

FACT FILE
Distance: 2 miles Height gain 140m / 450ft
Time: 1.5 hours
Start/Finish: Ardtoe west of Acharacle GR 628708 OS Sheet 40

47 BEINN BHREAC AND LOCH MOIDART

Many visit Castle Tioram, but few venture into the quiet hill country to the immediate east or explore the roadless southern section of Loch Moidart. This half day walk remedies these omissions and includes an optional short ascent of Beinn Bhreac 240m/ 788ft. This is an excellent viewpoint on a clear day looking to Beinn Resipol beyond Loch Shiel, across Loch Moidart and the surrounding rugged Moidart hills. Although mostly on good paths, boots are essential as the central section is rough and often quite wet.

Take the narrow road signed for Dorlin off the A861 just north of Acharacle. Park in the car park at the road end near Castle Tioram and walk back along the road for half a mile. Cross a stile over the road from a phone box and follow the clear path beside a small burn, cutting up through a deep craggy defile. Continue above the north side of a lochan surrounded by low moorland hills with a mass of bare rock slabs. At the foot of a short descent bear left at a path junction close to a second lochan. After a further quarter of a mile or so of gentle climbing, leave the path and cut up over the moorland slopes onto Beinn Bhreac, weaving easily between numerous small slabby outcrops. Deer tracks can assist through the heather. Deer are very likely to be seen along with many moorland birds although their camouflage is so good against the brown moorland that they may remain unobserved unless they move.

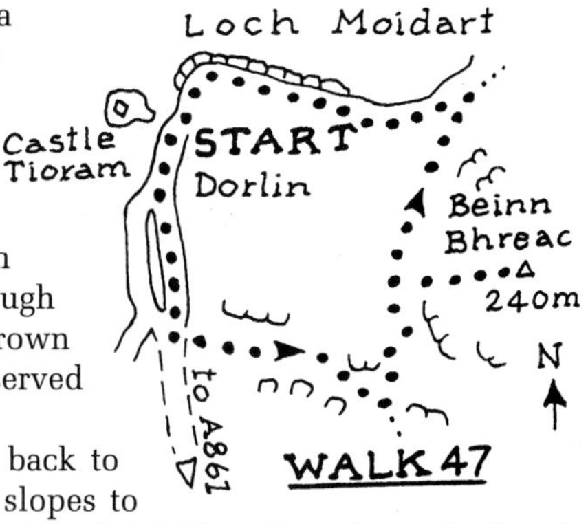

From the summit retrace your steps back to the path then continue down rather wet slopes to the attractive thinly wooded south shore of Loch Moidart. Just above the beach, turn left onto the well constructed path which rises and falls around the small craggy bays inhabited by grey herons and a host of smaller wading birds.

The walk finishes at Castle Tioram, pronounced 'cheerum'. It translates as 'Dry Castle', since it can be reached dryshod at low tide along a sandy causeway. Completed in 1353, it was home to 14 successive Macdonald of Clanranald clan chiefs and an important stronghold at the time of great feuding between the Lords of the Isles and the Kings of Scotland. Alan, the fourteenth chief, foresaw his own death whilst preparing to join the Earl of Mar's Jacobite army in 1715. He burnt the castle to prevent it falling into Hanovarian hands. The outer walls are remarkably well preserved. A display board in the car park shows what the interior would have looked like in its heyday.

FACT FILE
Distance: 5 miles Height gain 280m/ 919ft
Time: 3 – 4 hours
Public Transport: Kilchoan – Fort William and Mallaig – Acharacle buses pass within 2 miles of the start at Acharacle

48 SMIRISARY

This very short coastal stroll provides grandiose views for relatively little effort. The hardest part is negotiating the awkward single track road which leaves Glenuig past the inn and weaves for 1.5 miles beyond a shallow bay looking out across Samalaman Island.

From the road end just beyond a large parking area, a clear path signed for 'Smirisary' leads across a short stretch of moorland to the coast. After rain boots are essential although the boggiest sections are quite well paved. At a path junction above the sea, bear left downhill to the mix of scattered new but tastefully built holiday homes and the ruins of the old crofting settlement. Yet another reminder of the cruel Highland Clearances. The sheep remain, including some unusual breeds.

It is a wonderful place to potter around for an hour or two, following the sheep tracks and ascending heather and rocky knolls above the crashing Atlantic rollers. Steep hills of bare rock and heather end in smaller knolls above the impressive fretted coast of tilted rock strata. A quarter of a mile south of the houses, a burn has cut a sizeable gorge. The vistas extend westward to Ardnamurchan and north to the Arisaig Peninsula whilst to seaward lie the Isles of Rum, Eigg and Canna.
10 – 15 minute walk to Smirisary
On schooldays Acharacle – Mallaig buses pass through Glenuig

49 THE ASCENT OF ROIS- BHEINN 2893ft / 882m & AN STAC 2670 ft / 874m

The wild lonely region bounded by Lochs Shiel, Eilt and Ailort, tends to be unfashionable walking country without a Munro to its name. A line of 6 Corbetts however provide excellent ridge walking with views to match anything the equally rough and more well known Knoydart Munros can offer just to the north. Exceptionally fit walkers can traverse them all in one day. More realistically, a superb walk encircles the peaks of Coire a' Bhuiridh starting from Inverailort to the north, traversing Druim Fiaclach round to An Stac. This however still entails 5400 feet of ascent, which is beyond the capabilities of many walkers.

Shapely Rois-Bheinn and An Stac provide the grandest viewpoints of the bunch and can be combined in an easier round. On a clear day, the seaward prospect beyond Loch Ailort to the Inner Hebrides is breathtaking and one of the finest vistas along the fretted west coast.

Park in one of the good lay-bys along Loch Ailort between Roshven and Alisary then follow the scenic A861

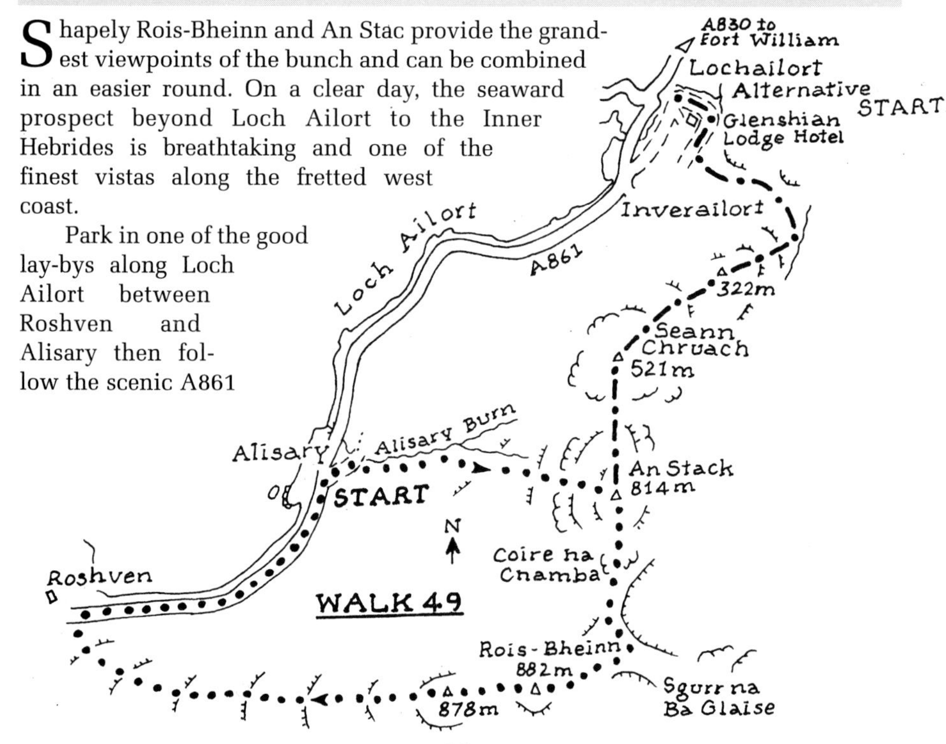

road north along the island studded and rocky bay. At Alisary some 4.5 miles south of Lochailort, a gated track leads in a short distance to the Alisary Burn. Just before the stone bridge turn right and follow the clear but narrow and often wet path running up the left side of the forest fence on the south bank of the boisterous and entertaining river. (If the burn is in spate, it is worth a visit by those not planning to climb the mountains themselves). The path weaves up through silver birch saplings rising high above the sizeable and impressive gorge full of small falls. The path eventually fizzles out beyond the forest but continue into Coire na Cnamha beneath the western flanks of An Stac. The climb up to the cone shaped summit is steep but essentially grassy, weaving between numerous rocky outcrops. The steep trudge is offset by the increasingly extensive seaward panorama behind you.

The dramatic, broken northern cliffs of Rois-Bheinn and Sgurr na Ba Glaise are well seen as you descend a steep, rocky ridge southward from An Stac. From the col below, navigation is simplified as the remains of an old dyke lead steeply up to the Bealach an Fhiona, then more easily westward onto the summit of Rois-Bheinn (ross ven), *possibly 'the mountain of horses'* from the Norse or from the Gaelic, *ros, 'a headland'* given its position overlooking the sea. The views to Loch Sunart, Ardnamuchan, the Hebrides and Knoydart are even more superb from the lower west top, reached by an easy ridge still bearing the remains of the wall.

There are several options in descent. Kindest on the knees is to follow the straightforward, moderately graded, grassy west ridge all the way down to Roshven on Loch Ailort, then follow the road back towards Alisary. (For walkers just wishing to climb one peak, this ridge offers the easiest route both in ascent and descent). Alternatively, from the west top, skirt the last of the northern crags and descend steeply to the Alisary Burn, aiming for the top east corner of the forest, to pick up the path used in ascent.

For walkers relying purely on public transport, it is easiest to begin the ascent at Lochailort and take the track past the Glenshian Lodge Hotel. A path then heads through a small pass below Tom Odhar. Climb SW onto the rocky ground of Seann Chruach and follow the ridge steeply southward onto An Stac. One can use one of the aforementioned descent routes from the west top of Rois-Bheinn back down to the road and follow this along Loch Ailort to return to your start point (on schooldays a bus leaves from Roshven for Lochailort at 14.39 hours).

FACT FILE

Distance: 6.5 miles Height gain: 1194m / 3919ft

Time: 5 – 7 hours.

Start/Finish: A861 at Alisary GR 741795 (alternate Lochailort GR 768824)

Remarks: Apart from the easier west ridge of Rois-Bheinn, steep rocky ridges may cause problems under snow.

Public Transport: Good train and bus service Fort William to Mallaig stops at Lochailort.

Stalking: Roshven Estate, contact Colin Surnam, c/o Lochailort Post Office 01687 470200

If climbing from Inverailort, contact Inverailort estate 01687 470234

49A EASY OPTION – GLEN MOIDART

The steep southern slopes of Rois-Bheinn flank the peaceful and picturesque narrow U-shaped glacial valley of Glen Moidart. This can be reached by a minor road running east for 2 miles from the head of Loch Moidart. The lower glen is beautifully wooded and cloaked with rhododendrons clustering around the majestic river. A signed track bears off to the right, just before the road end parking area and leads past Loch nan Lochan into the more open upper glen where the wide river is surrounded by the craggy Moidart mountains cut by some attractive burns. The path climbs a little but the going is gentle throughout its 5 mile course. In its latter stages it can occasionally be boggy. Return the same way.

50 THE ARDNISH PENINSULA

Mainly on a good path, this relatively short, but invigorating, ascent explores part of the quiet Ardnish Peninsula, an area of low moorland hills sandwiched between beautiful Loch Nan Uamh and Loch Ailort. It affords ever changing and highly photogenic vistas both to landward and seaward towards the Inner Hebrides. An ideal outing for hillwalkers denied the higher summits by gale force winds.

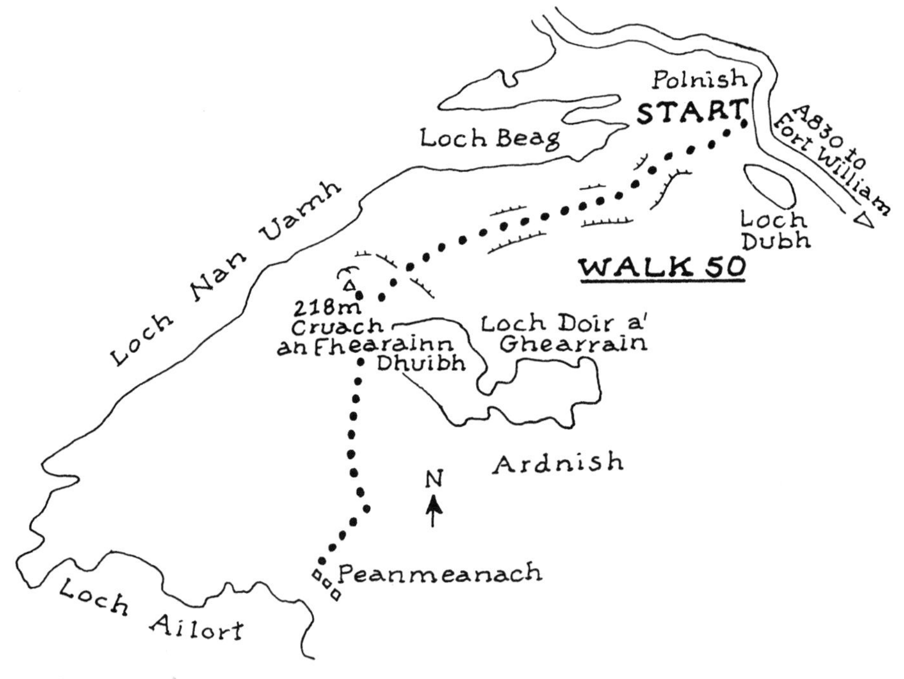

Park at the large layby just uphill of Polnish House, quarter of a mile north of Loch Dubh on the A830. Road improvements have rather spoilt the start of the path, a few yards south of the track to Polnish. It soon becomes very clear however and winds through stands of birch and alder, crossing the railway by charming Loch Dubh. Surrounded by bare slabby hills, the path now begins to climb through a scattering of trees winding above Loch Beag, a small rocky bay which is part of the large and complex Loch Nan Uamh. A profusion of primroses and anemones brighten the way in spring whilst butterwort fill the damper recesses in the rough, rocky path. Beyond the trees, the path emerges onto flatter moorland and undulates gently above Loch Nan Uamh with enthralling views to Eigg and the Rum Cuillin fronted by the Arisaig Peninsula. It is easy to see why Bonnie Prince Charlie chose this loch as a landing and embarkation point during the 1745-46 Jacobite Rebellion. A French ship could easily hide from English ships along such a fretted and difficult coastline.

On reaching a low pass, a wonderful panorama greets you across Loch Doir a' Ghearrain to the majestic Corbetts of Rois-Bheinn and An Stac. The path continues easily for another 1.25 miles, descending to the ruins and bothy at Peameanoch, an enchanting picnic spot above a small sandy cove overlooking the Sound of Arisaig towards Ardnamurchan. For the finest views however, include en route an ascent of Cruach an Fhearainn Duibh 218m / 715ft, easily ascended from the pass. A 10 minute climb up slopes of rough grass and heather between small outcrops of convoluted folded rocks gains the summit, perched airily above a precipitous western face. The incomparable combination of glistening lochs, island studded seas and lonely craggy mountains is magical.

It would be possible to make a circular walk returning from Peanmeanach to Polnish via the moorland hills on the eastern side of the peninsula overlooking Loch Ailort, but the ground is rough and complex and most walkers will prefer to retrace their steps.

FACT FILE

Distance: 7 miles Height gain: 1175ft/ 358m
Time: 3 – 4 hours
Start/Finish: Polnish House on A830 GR743835 OS Sheet 40
Public Transport: Fort William – Mallaig buses pass start

51 GLEN BEASDALE FALLS

Considering the generally wet climate of Moidart and Morar and the plethora of rivers, there are few readily accessible waterfalls of note to visit. An exception is Glen Beasdale just north of Loch Nan Uamh which boasts a series of small but attractive waterfalls, little more than a mile from the road; an ideal destination for a short walk when the weather is inclement and the water level high.

The walk begins on the north side of the Beasdale Burn, just beyond the road bridge on the A830 around the crown of a bend. (There is plenty of parking within quarter of a mile of the south side of the bridge). A path which is inclined to be rather wet initially, leads gently into the glen dotted with old deciduous woodland and flanked by steep sided slabby hills. After about 400 yards a very marshy patch has to be circumvented. Here the track bears to the left (ignore the distinct path going straight ahead) keeping to the left of small rock topped hillocks, before swinging back to run above and parallel with the river. Beyond a wide grassy strath, often teeming with deer, the river cascades in charming wee cataracts through a number of small rocky gorges lined with numerous bog plants and tenaciously clinging holly and birch trees. The path becomes drier and rises gently. About a mile from the road, the most obvious falls are reached. A series of waterslides tumble down interconnecting tilted rock strata for over 50 feet. There are other small falls both above and below here. None can be properly seen from the path. It is best to climb about 400 yards above the main falls on the path then cross the rough grass to reach the river and follow it back down to the lowest of the gorges. The path through the glen can easily be rejoined at any point.

Hillwalkers wishing to extend the outing outwith the stalking season, can follow the path right up the glen to the Bealach a' Mhama. The moorland hills rising to some 500 metres to the north of the pass, can be easily ascended for interesting views over the South and North Morar Peninsulas to Knoydart and the Moidart coast.

FACT FILE

Waterfalls walk 2.5 miles Height gain: 80m/262ft
Start/Finish: A830 north of Loch Nan Uamh GR 715852 OS Sheet 40
Public Transport: Beasdale rail station 600 yards to west, Mallaig buses pass start

52 LOCH MORAR WALKS

The minor road striking east from Morar village along Loch Morar, ends at the scattered housing of Bracorina. From here, several relatively easy, attractive, quiet walks are possible, well away from the crowds of Morar and Mallaig.

The shortest alternative explores some of the wild hinterland of the North Morar peninsula. Starting just across the bridge at the road end, a path heads ENE climbing gently from the delightful wooded shores of Loch Morar through heather and bracken to reach a moorland plateau dotted with numerous small lochans surrounded by grassy hillocks and rocky knolls. The path reaches a highpoint about 900 feet above Stoul from which there is a splendid view across Loch Nevis to the mountains of lonely Knoydart. Returning by the same route, one can enjoy the seaward view over the wooded island studded western corner of Loch Morar.
Distance: 5 miles, Height gain 900 ft/274m, Time: 2.5 – 3 hours
Remarks: The path is often inclined to be rather wet and boggy and gaiters are recommended in addition to boots.

The second alternative from Bracorina is longer but much drier underfoot and requires relatively little climbing. From the road end, an excellent undulating track hugs the shoreline of Loch Morar eastward to South Tarbert Bay, allowing for panoramic vistas across the loch and eastward to a jumble of rugged peaks. Fans of the recent film 'Rob Roy' may well spot some familiar scenes en route. From the small bay, a track heads northward across the narrow neck of the North Morar

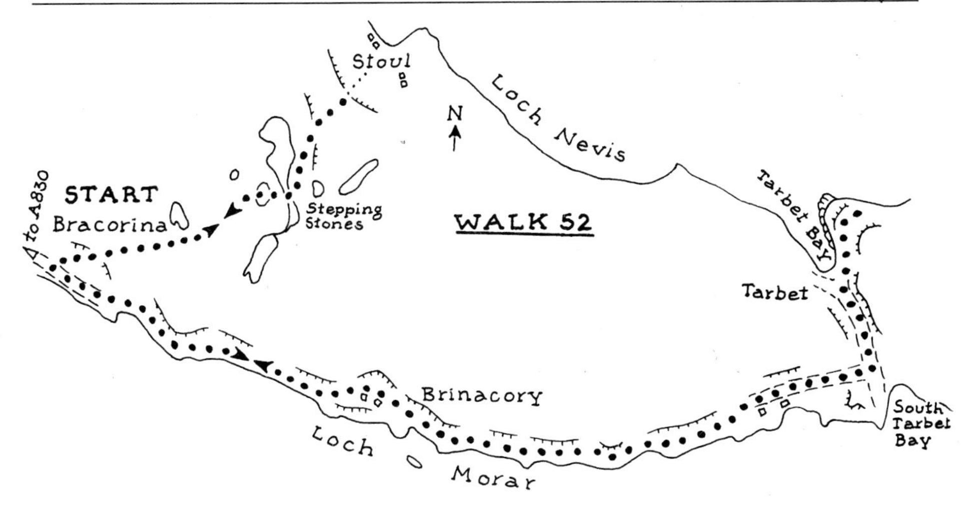

peninsula, to reach Tarbert Bay on Loch Nevis. A path continues above the eastern side of the bay before swinging eastward above Loch Nevis, affording views of dramatic Knoydart. For more extensive panoramas (including the sharply pointed Sgurr na Ciche), quit the path and take to the high ground on your right. Again it is advisable to return by your outward route as the hinterland of the peninsula gives rough, pathless going.
Distance optional: To Tarbert Bay return 10 – 11 miles, Time: 4 – 5 hours

53 MALLAIGMORE, CRUACH MHALAIG AND CARN A' GHOBHAIR

High circular scenic walks are available from Mallaig, catering for all abilities. All begin by following the excellent path from East Bay on the south side of Mallaig harbour. A circular wooden board with very faded writing marks the start, to the immediate left of the house named 'Tigh na Craig'. Initially paved, it climbs quite steeply for a short way beside a flower filled ditch, with views out across the bay towards Skye and Rum. The gradient soon eases and climbs steadily into a small narrow glen with occasional glimpses to Eigg. From a high point of around 250 feet, the path descends easily to the scattered houses at Mallaigvaig. Views open out northward to Loch Nevis and Knoydart. To the right, there are traces of 'lazy beds', a system of trenches once used by far from lazy crofters to drain the cultivated strips. It was here that Bonnie Prince Charlie landed after 12 weeks in the Outer Hebrides and Skye, a hunted fugitive searching in vain for a vessel to return him to France after Culloden.

The track continues for a further 0.75 mile above the rocky coast to the cove at Mallaigmore. One must then return to Mallaigvaig from where the return to Mallaig can be varied by following the road with superb vistas to the Inner Hebrides. There is one short sharp climb, thereafter it is easy.
3 miles: Height gain 350 feet/107m: Time 1.5 hours

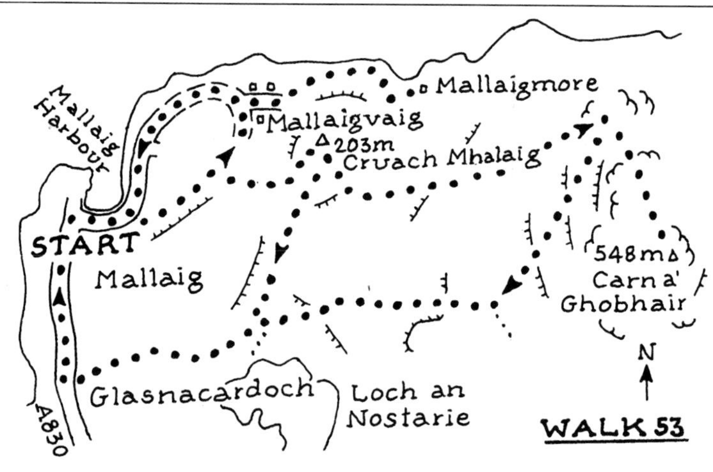

Start/ Finish: Mallaig Harbour OS Sheet 40 GR 679968
Public Transport: Mallaig is well served by buses and trains from Fort William

The more energetic walker can include an ascent of **Cruach Mhalaig 664ft / 203m,** a rounded hill overlooking Mallaigvaig. It can be climbed directly from the houses but this is very steep. Much easier is to go through a gate on the right from the high point of the path from Mallaig before reaching the hamlet. Traverse the grassy slopes to the south, eventually swinging round north eastward to approach the hill from its easier angled and grassier southern side. Wonderful vistas extend to the Hebrides, along the Moidart coast to Ardnamurchan, southward over attractive wooded island studded lochs and the wild mountains of Knoydart fronted by Loch Nevis.

There are numerous options in descent. The quickest option is to return towards Mallaigvaig. Alternatively head south for about 400 yards before swinging round into the valley of a small burn flowing northward to Mallaigmore, from where the coastal path can be gained. For a longer, more varied walk, descend SSE across the moorland to Loch an Nosterie from where a path leads to Glasnacardoch and the main road, some 0.75 mile along the coast from Mallaig.
Distance returning via Mallaigmore 3.75 miles (via Glasnacardoch 4.5 miles)
Height gain: 800 ft/ 243m
Time: 2 - 3 hours

Experienced hillwalkers climbing Cruach Mhalaig can continue onto **Carn a' Ghobhair 1794ft/ 548m,** 2 miles to the south east, from where the prospect is even more breathtaking. It is a steep, very rocky peak with only the north ridge offering a reasonable approach.

From Cruach Mhalaig, head south for about 500 yards then turn eastward climbing steadily over moorland to reach the well defined north ridge. This is fairly gentle in the main apart from 2 short steep sections and is straightforward in good conditions. It is not recommended in high winds and may be tricky under snow.

From the airy summit retrace your steps down the north ridge before heading SE down gentle moorland slopes to gain the aforementioned path, descending past Loch an Nosterie and so on down to the road at Glasnacardoch.

Distance: 8 miles Height Gain: 2200ft/ 670m
Time: 4 – 5 hours

54 ASCENT OF SGURR AN UTHA 796m/ 2612ft

'The peak of the udder' is one of a very rocky group of hills lying close to Glenfinnan. On a clear day, your reward for the relatively short ascent is one of the finest summit panoramas from any Corbett. Given the roughness of much of the ground and pathless upper section, it should not be undertaken lightly in either hillfog or under winter conditions.

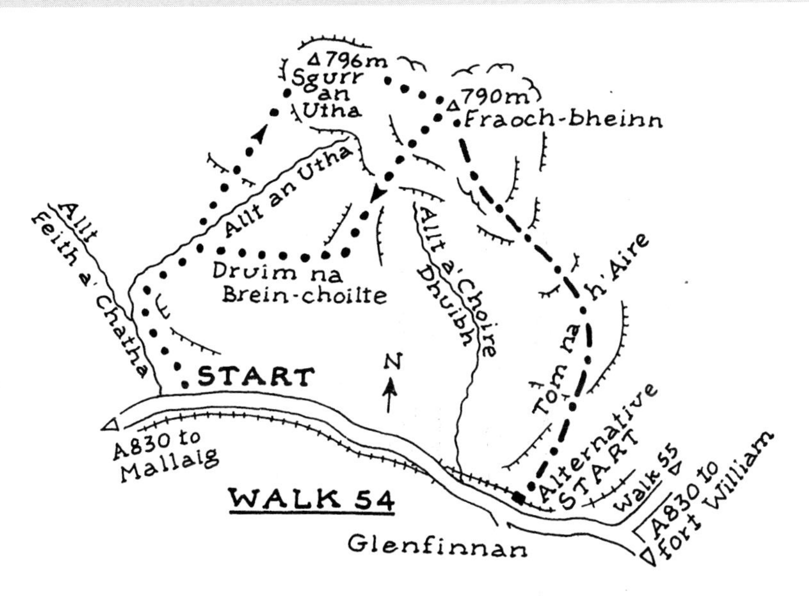

About 1.5 miles west of Glenfinnan rail station, a bridge on the A830 spans the Allt Feith a' Chatha (parking is available on the west side). To the east of the bridge, a forest track not marked on the map, heads northward above the east bank of the river. It soon leaves the forest and debouches onto open hillside above the Allt an Utha, swinging north eastward and climbing steadily towards Druim na Brein-chaille. Having gained some height, cross over the stream, abandoning the track to gain the south west ridge of Sgurr an Utha. *Note that if the water level is high, Allt an Utha can be awkward to cross. It may be necessary to leave the track much earlier and use the bridge at the confluence of the Allt Feith a' Chatra and Allt an Utha. The latter can then be followed to gain the SW ridge.* The extremely

rocky ridge leads to a summit of upended mica schist, situated airily above precipitous slopes dropping northward to the Allt a' Chaol-ghlinne. The superlative vistas encompass remote Loch Beoraid, through the dramatic glacial gash between the Streaps and Sgurr Thuilm to Loch Arkaig and over innumerable wild hills to Knoydart and equally rough Moidart.

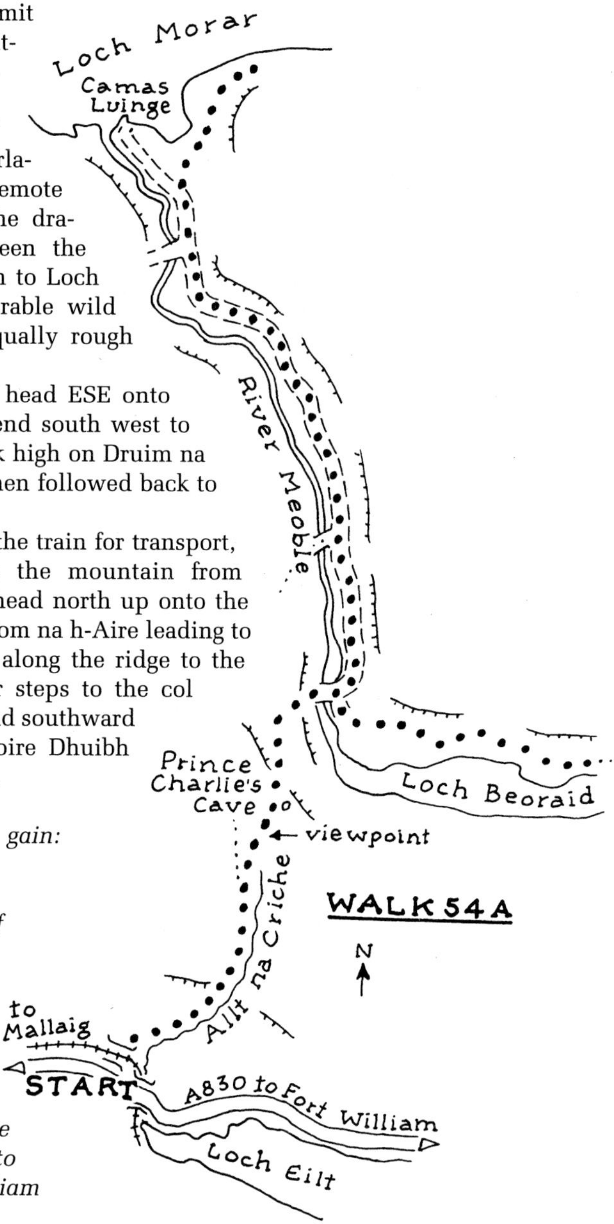

To vary the descent, head ESE onto Fraoch-bheinn then descend south west to the start of the forest track high on Druim na Breinn-choille which is then followed back to the road.

If you are relying on the train for transport, the easiest approach to the mountain from Glenfinnan Station is to head north up onto the steep and rocky ridge of Tom na h-Aire leading to Fraoch-bheinn. Continue along the ridge to the Corbett then retrace your steps to the col between the two hills. Head southward following the Allt a' Choire Dhuibh back down to Glenfinnan.

FACT FILE

Distance: 5 miles Height gain: 2462ft/ 750m
Time: 4 hours
Start/Finish: A830 west of Glenfinnan OS sheet 40 GR 875817
Stalking: Glenfinnan estate stalker tel. 01397 722203
Public transport: there are good rail/bus services to Glenfinnan from Fort William

54A *EASIER OPTION – LOCH BEORAID AND LOCH MORAR*

This much shorter climb still enables one to explore the remote heart of the wild South Morar region around Loch Beoraid with the option to continue on to beautiful Loch Morar.

Beyond the western end of Loch Eilt, the A830 turns briefly northward. In 0.25 mile a narrow path leaves the road to the left of the driveway serving the house named 'Craiglea'. The path goes under the railway on the right hand bank of the Allt na Criche and follows the burn uphill. In just over a mile, after 750 feet of climbing, a small boggy plateau is reached above the western end of the highly photogenic Loch Beoraid which few visitors ever see. A cave lying below the path was used by Bonnie Prince Charlie whilst a hunted fugitive after Culloden.

It is easy to lose the path temporarily amongst the bog. Those wishing to go further may have to take to the higher ground on the left, rejoining the path a little further on. The path now descends easily to the River Meoble. Having crossed the bridge, one can either turn right and follow the rough path above the north shore of Loch Beoraid or turn left along a good track heading northward to Loch Morar. On reaching the small bay of Camas Luinge, the views of Loch Morar can be greatly extended by taking to the higher ground east of the bay. Although circular walks are possible in this area, the very rough nature of the ground will deter all but the hardiest of walkers and most will prefer to return by the outward route.
Distance optional: to the viewpoint over Loch Beoraid and return, 2.25 miles with height gain 750 ft. To Loch Morar and return 9.25miles, height gain 1550ft.

55 THE TRAVERSE OF SGURR THUILM 3164ft / 963m & SGURR NAN COIREACHAN 3136ft / 956m

This is a grand horseshoe ridge walk, traversing two dramatically situated Munros, readily accessible for those staying in the Fort William area. They stand amidst a remote and rugged jumble of peaks overlooking lonely Lochs Morar and Arkaig.

The easiest approach is from the National Trust car park at Glenfinnan on the A830 road to Mallaig; a beautiful and historic spot at the head of Loch Shiel. Here, Bonnie Prince Charlie raised his standard in 1745 and began his ill fated quest to seize the British crown on behalf of his exiled father. A wide rough track follows the gentle floor of Glen Finnan on the west bank of the river, passing beneath the spectacular engineering feat of the curving railway viaduct built in 1899. In good weather, it is a bonny and peaceful glen with deciduous trees lining the river banks and steep, knobbly, craggy hills on all sides, with increasingly afforested lower slopes.

Some 2.25 miles on, the track fords the Allt a'Chaol-ghlinne at Corryhully then continues for another mile alongside the River Finnan. Cross the Allt Coire a'Bheithe and head steeply up the right hand grassy flanks of Druim Coire a'Bheithe, easily turning the occasional small rocky outcrop. Once onto the crest

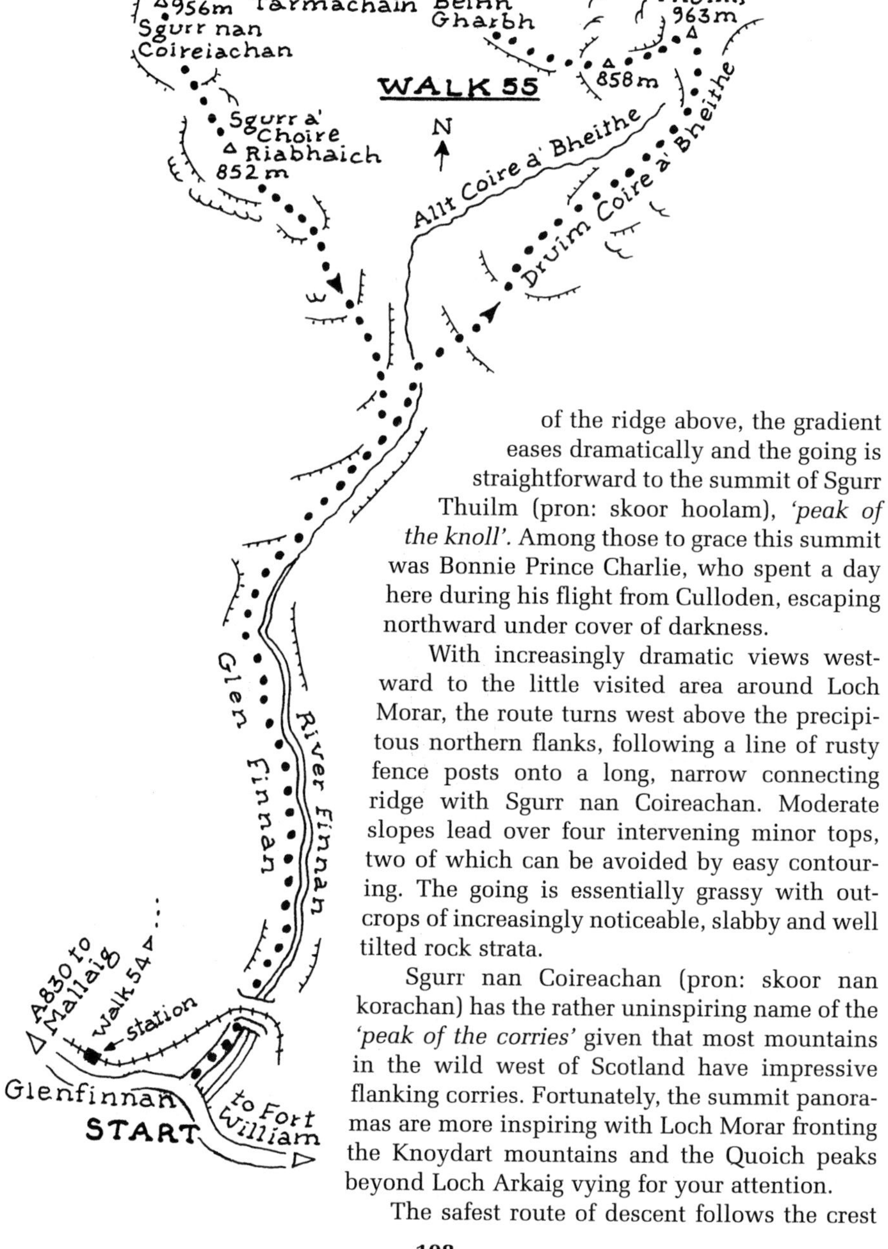

of the ridge above, the gradient eases dramatically and the going is straightforward to the summit of Sgurr Thuilm (pron: skoor hoolam), *'peak of the knoll'*. Among those to grace this summit was Bonnie Prince Charlie, who spent a day here during his flight from Culloden, escaping northward under cover of darkness.

With increasingly dramatic views westward to the little visited area around Loch Morar, the route turns west above the precipitous northern flanks, following a line of rusty fence posts onto a long, narrow connecting ridge with Sgurr nan Coireachan. Moderate slopes lead over four intervening minor tops, two of which can be avoided by easy contouring. The going is essentially grassy with outcrops of increasingly noticeable, slabby and well tilted rock strata.

Sgurr nan Coireachan (pron: skoor nan korachan) has the rather uninspiring name of the *'peak of the corries'* given that most mountains in the wild west of Scotland have impressive flanking corries. Fortunately, the summit panoramas are more inspiring with Loch Morar fronting the Knoydart mountains and the Quoich peaks beyond Loch Arkaig vying for your attention.

The safest route of descent follows the crest

of the SE ridge, down steep grassy slopes, wending a way between a maze of small crags. A short gentle ascent gains Sgurr Choire Riabhaich which has precipitously steep rocky flanks, avoided by keeping to the grassier crest as you continue steeply down south eastward. This eventually brings broader and easier slopes. Some 600 ft above the floor of Glen Finnan, an excellent stalkers' track on the east side of the ridge leads down into the glen and the track of your outward route.

FACT FILE

Distance: 13 miles Height gain: 4000ft / 1200m
Time: 6 – 8 hours
Start/Finish: Car park Glenfinnan OS Sheet 40 GR905809
Remarks: Good navigational skills needed in hillfog. The descent can be difficult under snow.
Stalking season: Contact Glenfinnan Estate Stalker Tel. 01397 722203
Public Transport: Glenfinnan is well served by Fort William to Mallaig buses and trains.

EASY OPTIONS

The first 2.25 miles along Glen Finnan are on very gentle track and make for an easy and attractive glen walk (see above).

Similarly, 4.25 miles eastward along the main road from Glenfinnan Monument, an easy track leads several miles northward up Gleann Fionnlighe on the east bank of an attractive wide river, surrounded by a mass of silver birches, backed by rugged hills. In springtime, a host of playful lambs will provide the local entertainment, but be sure to keep any dogs on leads.

56 ASCENT OF SGURR GHIUBHSACHAIN 849m/2784ft & SGORR CRAOBH A' CHAORAINN 775m/ 2544ft

For seasoned hillwalkers the traverse of these two superb rocky peaks near Glenfinnan makes a magnificent outing, though it is not one to be taken lightly owing to their steep and craggy nature. Keep them for a clear day when route selection will be relatively straightforward and the views breathtaking.

Approximately 1.6 miles east of Glenfinnan Monument, a well surfaced forestry road leads off the A830 and heads southward for 200 yards to a river bridge (ample parking within the vicinity). Following the sign for 'Polloch 15 miles', turn right. The road soon rises gently for 200 feet providing a fine view east to Ben Nevis through gaps in the delightful flanking curtain of birch, alder, willow and Scots pine which effectively hide the monotonous conifer plantations. A gentle descent brings Loch Shiel and beautiful views of the surrounding rugged hills dwarfing the Glenfinnan monument and railway viaduct.

Follow the road along the loch shore for another 2 miles to Guesachan Cottage at the foot of the north ridge of Sgurr Ghiubhsachain. To avoid the initially very steep and craggy ground, gain height above the west bank of the Allt Coire Ghiubhsachain before heading up onto the ridge itself. The route weaves steeply

between rocky bluffs where scramblers can find some optional entertainment. The going eases briefly beyond the shoulder of Meall a' Choire Churuinn before another steep climb gains a small subsidiary top. The true summit of *'the peak of the fir-wood'* lies along a short, easy ridge to the south west; a fine craggy perch overlooking Loch Shiel with a superb array of wild mountains on all fronts.

Taking care, descend steeply ESE over grassy and slabby ground to reach easier going around the head of Coire Ghiubhsachain and the relatively gentle though often slabby SW ridge of Sgorr Craobh a' Chaorainn. The rocky summit of *'rowan tree peak'* is airily situated above a steep west face and is best approached by keeping to the east side of the ridge towards the top. When you can draw yourself away, descend NE over Meall na Cuartaige; any small rock outcrops are easily turned. Just above splendid mixed forest, a path is joined along the west bank of the Allt na Cruaiche, a vibrant river in spate. Its tributary, the Allt Coire a' Leacaich is also lively and if the water level is high can be awkward to cross. The path beyond continues down the wild and attractive glen for 2 miles to your starting point.

FACT FILE

Distance: 11.5 miles Height gain 1100m./ 3610 ft
Time: 8 hours
Start/Finish: Near Callop on A830 road, OS Sheet 40 GR 925794
Remarks: Navigationally testing in hillfog, and difficult under snow.
Stalking: Cona Glen Estate restrict access 15 August – 20 October. Tel. the stalker 01855 841304 or West Highland Estates Office 01397 702433
Public Transport: Fort William – Mallaig buses pass the start. Trains stop at Glenfinnan.

EASY ALTERNATIVE

The first section of the walk as intimated above, is gentle and on a good track, providing an easy and very beautiful walk or cycle. The 2 miles to Glenfinnan are recommended with the option to continue along Loch Shiel for upto 13 miles to Polloch. No special footwear is necessary.

APPENDIX

USEFUL TELEPHONE NUMBERS

MOUNTAIN WEATHERCALL – 0891 500441
CLIMBLINE 0891 333198

TOURIST INFORMATION OFFICES

Ballachulish *(April – Oct)* – 01855 811296
Craignure (Mull) *(April – Oct)* – 01680 812377
Fort William *(all year)* – 01397 703781)
Kilchoan *(April – Oct)* – 01972 510222
Mallaig *(April – Oct)* – 01687 462170
Oban *(all year)* – 01631 563122
Spean Bridge *(April – Oct)* – 01397 712576
Strontian *(April – Oct)* – 01967 402131
Tobermory *(all year)* – 01688 302182

YOUTH HOSTELS

Glencoe *(all year)* 01855 811219
Glen Nevis *(all year)* 01397 702336
Oban *(open all year except 27 Dec – 4 Jan)* 01631 562025
Tobermory *(21 Mar - 27 Oct)* 01688 302481

SKI-ING

Glencoe 15 runs, 6 lifts
Ski Hotline *(road & snow conditions)* 01891 654 658
Ski Call *(Met Office's ski service)* 01891 500795
Ski School 01397 750825

Nevis Range 18 runs all levels, 9 lifts, dry slope
Ski Hotline 01891 654660
Ski Call 01891 500799
Ski School 01397 705825

SCOTTISH TOURIST BOARD

23 Ravelston Terrace, Edinburgh
0131 332 2433
For details of :
Golfing holidays
Leaflets on Pony Trekking & Riding Centres in Scotland,
Yachting Charter Firms, anchorages & other water sports

ROYAL YACHTING ASSOCIATION

Caledonia House, South Gyle, Edinburgh
0131 317 7388

ANGLING

Central Scotland Anglers Association 53 Fernieside Crescent, Edinburgh
0131 664 4685
Scottish Anglers National Association 307 West George Street, Glasgow
0141 221 7206
Scottish Federation for Course Angling Tigh na Fleurs, Hill o' Gryfe Road, Bridge of Weir, Renfrewshire
01505 612580
The Scottish Federation of Sea Anglers 18 Ainslie Place, Edinburgh
0131 225 7611